Berlitz® WITHDRAWN
ОM STOCK

Hong Kong

Front cover: A traditional junk in
Hong Kong bay
Right. Clear transport signage

Man Mo Temple. The air here is always heady with incense. See page 32.

Tian Tan Buddha on Lantau. This is the world's tallest seated bronze statue of the Buddha. See page 61.

New Territories. See the dramatic scenery, fringed with numerous secluded beaches. See page 51.

Glittering skyscrapers. Central district is home to an array of bold, modern structures. See page 26.

Sheung Wan. Explore the fascinating streets here and a way of life that is fast disappearing. See page 33.

Cheung Chau. Step down a gear on this small, laid-back outlying island. See page 63.

Shopping. Day or night, indulging in retail therapy is an experience not to be missed. See page 79.

The Star Ferry. The most exciting way to cross Victoria Harbour is on this iconic craft. See page 25.

Victoria Peak. A ride to the top on the famous Peak Tram provides some stunning views over the city. See page 28.

Man Fat Tze. Brave the steep climb to visit the Monastery of 10,000 Buddhas. See page 57.

A PERFECT DAY

9.30am Markets

From Queen's Road, walk through Central's Gage Street and Graham Street outdoor food markets to see the freshest selection of fruit, vegetables, meat, fish and seafood in town. If food isn't your thing, but shopping is, Central's shops start opening from 10am.

10.45am Dim sum

Head to City Hall to join the locals for dim sum in Maxim's restaurant, which has harbour views. Stop any trolley and choose from the bamboo steamers. Favourites include the white *ha gow* (shrimp) or yellow *siu mai* (pork and shrimp).

11.30am To Kowloon

Catch an MTR to TST East to visit the Museum of History in Chatham Road or head to Mongkok and Yau Ma Tei street markets.

2.00pm Relaxing gardens

Go to Diamond Hill to visit one of the best Chinese-style gardens in Hong Kong at Nian Lin, before exploring the wooden Tang-style buildings at nearby Chi Lin nunnery. Lunch or afternoon tea is available at the delightful Chi Lin Vegetarian restaurant.

5.00pm Pampering

Relax and enjoy the views of Kowloon from Langham Place, Mong Kok's 41st floor Chuan Spa, which specialises in treatments based on traditional Chinese medicine. Everyone can attempt to realign their meridians and balance their ying and yang here, with the help of a massage.

中環
Central

IN HONG KONG

8.00pm City lights

Stop at the Central Ferry Pier for al fresco drinks at the eponymous Pier 7. Walk along the Central waterfront to Pier 3 and take in the lights of Two IFC and other Central buildings before taking a taxi or Central-Mid-Levels escalator up to SoHo.

10.00pm Big night out

Its easy to wander around SoHo, or along Wyndham Street and down through Lan Kwai Fong to find an open-fronted bar and join the crowds. The bar on the Fringe Club rooftop has plenty of space, or for live music, try the Peel Fresco Music Lounge (49 Peel Street).

7.00pm The harbour

The harbour must be seen by night, so it's back down to the TST waterfront, where you can either hop on the Star Ferry for a trip across the harbour or take the red-sailed Aqua Luna junk to the Clock Tower for a 45-minute cruise to Central.

8.30pm Dinner options

Dinner in the SoHo area means dozens of restaurants and cuisines to choose from. There's something for everyone at the Peak Café (9–13 Shelley Street), which serves an eclectic international menu; La Pampa (32 Staunton Street) has some of the best steaks in town; and Enoteca (47 Elgin Street) has great Mediterranean style platters.

CONTENTS

INTRODUCTION

Exciting, mysterious, glamorous – these words have described Hong Kong for over a century. With its vibrant atmosphere and bustle day and night, Hong Kong is an intoxicating place. There is no doubt that Hong Kong is crowded – it has one of the world's greatest population densities. But it is also efficient, with inexpensive public transport and taxis, and, for such a crowded place, it is safe, and has plenty of green peaceful places to escape to, away from the skyscrapers and traffic fumes. The shopping never ends – there's always another inviting spot just down the street. For visitors, Hong Kong is easy to get around with English is spoken in tourist areas, while the food continually surpasses its reputation.

A new era

On 1 July 1997 the British Crown Colony of Hong Kong reverted to Chinese sovereignty as a Special Administrative Region of the People's Republic of China. Today Hong Kong remains a capitalist enclave with its laws and rights intact, and China has promised that Hong Kong will continue in this fashion for at least 50 years. Beijing's declared policy of maintaining Hong Kong's prosperity and stability makes sense. Hong Kong has long been China's handiest window on the West, and the city is unrivalled in its commercial know-how and managerial expertise. Around the time of the transition there was much speculation about how things would change. But, in fact, once news of the handover vanished from the front pages, the people of Hong Kong returned to their usual topics of conversation: the economy and the price of housing.

Wan Chai at night

There have been changes, of course, many of them due to economic progress, new construction and other factors that influence cities all over the world. And there's not a great deal of Britain left. Establishments are no longer preceded by the world 'Royal', Queen Elizabeth has vanished from the coinage, and the Union flag has been replaced by that of China and the new Hong Kong flag with its bauhinia flower. You're far more likely to hear Mandarin on Hong Kong's streets than English now. Meanshile, it has become much easier for mainlanders to get travel permits to the SAR, and with the increasing affluence of many across the border there has been a surge in the number of Chinese tourists, who now make up the biggest group by nationality – 40.7 million visited in 2013. And in terms of expats, there are now more Americans working in Hong Kong than Brits.

People and customs

With a population of over seven million and a total area of just over 1,100 sq km (425 sq miles), housing is one of Hong Kong's perennial nightmares. To alleviate the problem, the government has become the city's major landlord with the construction of massive residential blocks. Though they have every modern facility, new flats average an internal floor area per person of only around 11 sq m (120 sq ft). Whole cities have been created in the New Territories, although the unimaginative architecture

Fragrant Harbour

Hong Kong's name is derived from the Cantonese phrase for 'Fragrant Harbour' – *Heung Gong*. The evocative name probably derives from the trade in locally-grown incense wood, which once thrived in what is now Aberdeen. Another theory ascribes the name to the bauhinia, an aromatic flower which is native to the region and is now the logo of the Hong Kong administration.

of these towns has been criticised.

Of Hong Kong's population, 95 percent are of Chinese descent. The majority are Cantonese, born in Hong Kong, or from South China, but there are immigrants from all over China. The Chinese people are often described as hardworking and pragmatic, attributes that have contributed immensely to Hong Kong's success. There are many stories of refugees who arrived with nothing in their pockets, set up a small pavement stall, worked diligently until they had their own shop, and then expanded it into a modest chain.

Making offerings at Wong Tai Sin temple

Old customs are still followed: fate and luck are taken very seriously, and astrologers and fortune-tellers do a steady business. Before a skyscraper can be built, a *feng shui* investigation must take place to ensure that the site and the building will promote health, harmony, and prosperity. Gambling is a passion, whether it be cards, mahjong, the lottery or the horses. Hong Kong has two major racecourses as well as an intensive off-course betting system for punters, and at the weekend the ferries to Macau are crowded with people on their way to the many casinos located there.

What to see

Sightseeing in Hong Kong starts at sea level with the enthralling water traffic – a mix of freighters, ferries, tugs, junks and yachts. Views of the city and the harbour are panoramic. From

A view of the harbour

the heights of Victoria Peak, or from skyscrapers and hotels, the views are especially exciting at night when the horizon comes alive in a blaze of lights.

The business and financial centre and the soaring architecture are on Hong Kong Island. Across Victoria Harbour, connected by the Star Ferry and MTR underground railway, is the Kowloon peninsula with its hotels, nightlife, and almost non-stop shopping. Beyond, in the New Territories, are a mixture of high-rise towns, the world's second-busiest container port, ancient walled villages, country parks and farms. Hong Kong's other, less developed islands, Lantau, Lamma and Cheung Chau, provide getaways. You can also take a ferry to Macau to find an entirely different kind of city, a rare blend of Chinese and Iberian culture.

It's anyone's guess what may happen in the future, but for now Hong Kong bristles with energy and ambition, and for the visitor, this beautiful city is an exhilarating experience.

A BRIEF HISTORY

In the popular mind, the history of Hong Kong, long the point of entry to China for Westerners, begins in 1841 with the British occupation of the territory. However, it would be wrong to dismiss the long history of the region itself. Archaeologists today are working to uncover Hong Kong's past, which stretches back thousands of years. You can get a glimpse into that past at Lei Cheng Uk Han Museum's 1,600-year-old burial vault on the mainland just north of Kowloon (see page 49). In 1992, when construction of the airport on Chek Lap Kok began, a 2,000-year-old village, Pak Mong, was discovered, complete with artefacts that indicated a sophisticated rural society. An even older Stone Age site was discovered on Lamma Island in 1996.

While Hong Kong remained a relative backwater in its early days, nearby Guangzhou (Canton) was developing into a great trading city with connections in India and the Middle East. By AD900, the Hong Kong islands had become a lair for pirates preying on the shipping in the Pearl River Delta and causing a major headache for burgeoning Guangzhou; small bands of pirates were still operating into the early years of the 20th century.

In the meantime, the mainland area was being settled by incomers, the 'Five Great Clans': Tang, Hau, Pang, Liu and Man. First to arrive was the Tang clan, which established a number of walled villages in the New Territories

Time travel

The *Hong Kong Story* at the Hong Kong Museum of History is the best way for a visitor to experience the territory's past. For just HK$10, you can travel from a point 400 million years ago to the 1997 handover. Exhibits are richly displayed and include replicas of an 18th-century fishing junk and a 1960s cinema.

that still exist today. You can visit Kat Hing Wai and Lo Wai, where the old village walls are still intact. Adjacent to Lo Wai is the Tang Chung Ling Ancestral Hall, built in the 16th century, and which is still the centre of clan activities to this day.

The first Europeans to arrive in the Pearl River Delta were the Portuguese, who settled in Macau in 1557 and had a monopoly on trade between Asia, Europe and South America for several centuries. As Macau developed into the greatest port in the East, it also became a base for Jesuit missionaries; it was later a haven for persecuted Japanese Christians. While Christianity was not a great success in China, it made local headway, as can be seen today in the numerous Catholic churches in Macau's historic centre.

The British arrive

The British established their presence in the area after Emperor Kangxi of the Qing Dynasty opened trade on a limited basis in Guangzhou (Canton) at the end of the 17th century. Trading began smoothly enough, but soon became subject to increasing restrictions, and all foreigners were faced with the attitude expressed by Emperor Qianlong at Britain's first attempt to open direct trade with China in 1793: 'We possess all things,' said the emperor, 'I set no value on objects strange or ingenious, and have no use for your country's manufactures.'

Moreover, China would accept nothing but silver bullion in exchange for its goods, so Britain had to look for a more abundant commodity to square its accounts. Around the end of the 18th century the traders found a solution: opium was the wonder drug that would solve the problem. Grown in India, it was delivered to Canton, and while China outlawed the trade in 1799, local Cantonese officials were always willing to look the other way for 'squeeze money' (a term still used in Hong Kong).

In 1839 the emperor appointed the incorruptible Commissioner Lin Tse-hsu to stamp out the smuggling of 'foreign mud'. Lin's crackdown was severe. He demanded that the British merchants in Canton surrender their opium stores, and to back up his ultimatum he laid siege to the traders, who, after six tense weeks, surrendered over 20,000 chests of opium. To Queen Victoria, Lin addressed a famous letter, pointing out the harm the 'poisonous drug' did to China, and asking for an end to the opium trade; his arguments are unanswerable but the lofty, though heartfelt, tone of the letter shows how unprepared the Chinese were to negotiate with the West in realistic terms.

Emperor Kangxi opened trade in Guangzhou on a limited basis

The Opium Wars

A year later, in June 1840, came the British retaliation, beginning the first of the so-called Opium Wars. After a few skirmishes and much negotiation, a peace agreement was reached. Under the Convention of Chuenpi, Britain was given the island of Hong Kong (where it had been anchoring its ships for decades), and on 26 January 1841, Hong Kong was proclaimed a British colony.

The peace plan achieved at Chuenpi was short-lived. Both Peking and London repudiated the agreement, and fighting resumed. This time the British forces, less than 3,000 strong but in possession of superior weapons and tactics, outfought the Chinese. Shanghai fell and Nangking was threatened. In the

Treaty of Nanking (1842) China was compelled to open five of its ports to foreign economic and political penetration, and even to compensate the opium smugglers for their losses. Hong Kong's status as a British colony and a free port was confirmed.

In the aftermath of the Opium Wars, trade in 'foreign mud' was resumed at a level even higher than before, although it ceased in 1907. Opium-smoking continued openly in Hong Kong until 1946; it was abolished by the Communist government in mainland China in 1949.

19th century commerce and prosperity

The first governor of Hong Kong, Sir Henry Pottinger, predicted it would become 'a vast emporium of commerce and wealth'. Under his direction, Hong Kong began its march towards prosperity. It was soon flourishing; with its natural harbour that attracted ships, Hong Kong leaped to the forefront as a base for trade. Both the population and the economy began to grow steadily. A surprise was the sizable number of Chinese who chose to move to the colony.

In the meantime, the opening of Hong Kong was the last blow to Macau's prosperity. Inroads had already been made by the arrival of the Dutch, and Macau's loss to them of the profitable Japanese trade. From then on, up until its 21st-century comeback as Asia's gambling capital, Macau sank into relative obscurity.

Despite the differences between the Chinese majority and the European minority, relations were generally cordial. Sir John Francis Davis, an early governor, disgusted with the squabbling of the English residents, declared: 'It is a much easier task to

An amusing isle

'Albert is so amused,' wrote Queen Victoria, 'at my having got the island of Hong Kong.' Her foreign secretary, Lord Palmerston, was not so amused; he dismissed Hong Kong as 'a barren island with hardly a house upon it'.

Causeway Bay in the mid-1800s

govern the 20,000 Chinese inhabitants of the colony than the few hundreds of English.'

There were a few incidents: On 15 January 1857, somebody added an extra ingredient to the dough at the colony's main bakery – arsenic. While the Chinese continued to enjoy their daily rice, the British, eating their daily bread, were dropping like flies. At the height of the panic, thousands of Chinese were deported from Hong Kong. No one ever discovered the identity or the motive of the culprits.

Conditions in the colony in the 19th century, however, did not favour the Chinese population. The British lived along the waterfront in Victoria (now Central) and on the cooler slopes of Victoria Peak. The Chinese were barred from these areas, and from any European neighbourhood. They settled in what is now known as the Western District. It was not uncommon for several families and their animals to share one room in crowded shantytowns. So it is not surprising that when bubonic plague struck in 1894, it took nearly 30 years to fully eradicate it. Today in parts of Western District, you can still wander narrow streets lined with small traditional shops selling ginseng, medicinal herbs, incense, tea and funeral objects.

In 1860, a treaty gave Britain a permanent beach-head on the Chinese mainland – the Kowloon peninsula, directly across Victoria harbour. In 1898, under the Convention of Peking, China leased the New Territories and 235 more islands to Britain for what then seemed an eternity – 99 years.

20th century intrusions

The colony's population has always fluctuated according to events beyond its borders. In 1911, when the Chinese

Trading houses

The Hong Kong of today owes its origins to the big trading houses or hongs of the 19th century. It was their top bosses or *taipans* who pressured the British government to secure a base to freely trade their opium and, once acquired, they were the driving force behind shaping the 'barren rock' into a successful trading port. Even today, places in Hong Kong bear the names of these big *taipans* as testament to their early power.

Rival *hongs* such as the Scottish Jardine, Matheson and England's Dent and Company were constantly squabbling among themselves. They were also at loggerheads with the government, which was chasing taxes and urging better treatment of the local Chinese. To avoid paying taxes many *taipans* became honoury consuls of foreign powers or sailed their ships under foreign flags.

Many of these hongs still exist today, successful because they diversified as Hong Kong's economy changed. Their offices are now hidden in the morass of skyscrapers, their interests spread widely through subsidiaries and some bought out by Chinese *taipans*. Although they no longer rule the roost, they still wield power from behind the scenes.

revolution overthrew the Manchus, refugees flocked to the safety of Hong Kong. Many arrived with nothing but the shirts on their backs, but they brought their philosophy of working hard and seizing opportunity. Hundreds of thousands more arrived in the 1930s when Japan invaded China. By the eve of World War II, the population was more than one and a half million.

A few hours after Japan's attack on the American fleet at Pearl Harbor in December 1941, a dozen Japanese battalions began an assault on Hong Kong; Hong Kong's minimal air force was destroyed on the airfield at Kai Tak within

Old and new buildings contrast in Hong Kong

five minutes. Abandoning the New Territories and Kowloon, the defenders retreated to Hong Kong island, hoping for relief which never came. They finally surrendered on Christmas Day in 1941. Survivors recall three and a half years of hunger and hardship under the occupation forces, who deported many Hong Kong Chinese to the mainland.

A number of Hong Kong's monuments were damaged: St John's Cathedral became a military club, the old governor's lodge on the Peak was burned down, and the commandant of the occupation forces rebuilt the colonial governor's mansion in Japanese style. At the end of World War II, Hong Kong's population was down to half a million, there was no industry, no fishing fleet, and few houses and public services remaining.

Post-war Hong Kong

China's civil war sent distressing echoes to Hong Kong. While the Chinese Communist armies drove towards the south, the flow of refugees into Hong Kong gathered force, and by the time the People's Republic of China was proclaimed in 1949, the total population of Hong Kong had grown to more than two million people. The fall of Shanghai in 1949 brought another flood of refugees, among them many wealthy people and skilled artisans, including the Shanghai industrialists who became the founders of Hong Kong's textile industry. Housing was now in desperately short supply. The problem became an outright disaster on Christmas Day in 1953. An uncontrollable fire devoured a whole city of squatters' shacks in Kowloon; 50,000 refugees were deprived of shelter.

The calamity spurred the government to launch an emergency programme of public-housing construction; spartan new blocks of flats put cheap and fireproof roofs over hundreds of thousands of heads. But this new housing was grimly overcrowded, and even a frenzy of construction couldn't keep pace with the increasing demand for living space. In 1962 the colonial authorities closed the border with China, but even this did not altogether stem the flow of refugees: the next arrivals were the Vietnamese boat people.

Hong Kong's economy boomed in the 1970s and 1980s, thanks largely to its role as China's trading partner, and as a result the standard of living in the colony rapidly improved.

Back to China

As 1997 drew near, it became clear that the Chinese government would not renew the 99-year lease on the New Territories. Negotiations began and in 1984, then British Prime Minister

Housing for the masses

Margaret Thatcher signed the Sino-British Joint Declaration. Britain confirmed the transfer of the New Territories and all Hong Kong to China in 1997. China declared Hong Kong a 'Special Administrative Region' and guaranteed its civil and social system for at least 50 years.

Although China's Basic Law promised that Hong Kong's existing laws and civil liberties would be upheld, many in Hong Kong were concerned. The British Nationality Act (1981) in effect prevented Hong Kong citizens from acquiring British citizenship, and thousands of people, anxious about their future, were prompted to apply for citizenship elsewhere, notably Canada and Australia. Some companies moved their headquarters out of Hong Kong.

Ironically, as the handover approached, the British granted the Hong Kong Chinese more political autonomy than they had since the colony was founded, including such democratic reforms as elections to the Legislative Council.

Hong Kong in the 21st century

The transfer of sovereignty occurred smoothly on 1 July 1997, but the Asian economic downturn hit Hong Kong hard in the years that followed. Then, in 2003, Severe Acute Respiratory Syndrome (SARs) killed 299 people in the city, but its people showed great resilience. In July 2003 more than half a million protestors marched peacefully to protest against proposed anti-subversion laws. The following year 200,000 marched and established the tradition of annual 'July 1st marches', calling for more democracy and voting reforms.Although Beijing has said the earliest possible date for direct elections for chief executive is 2017, and for Legislative Council – 2020, the 'pace of democracy' remains an issue. In 2013 Benny Tai Yiu-ting, Associate Professor of Law at the University of Hong Kong, launched a civil disobedience campaign and started the Occupy Central with Love and Peace movement to pressure Beijing and the SAR administration to introduce universal suffrage. The same year Hong Kong made international headlines as it offered a temporary refuge for the NSA whisleblower Edward Snowden.

Hong Kong's destiny has always been linked to the water

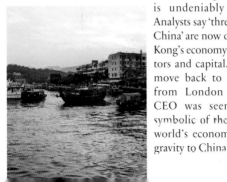

Despite these political issues, Hong Kong today is undeniably optimistic. Analysts say 'three flows from China' are now driving Hong Kong's economy – goods, visitors and capital. In 2010 the move back to Hong Kong from London of HSBC's CEO was seen as highly symbolic of the shift in the world's economic centre of gravity to China

Historical Landmarks

7th–9th centuries AD Probable arrival of the Tanka People. Chinese fortress constructed in Tuen Mun.

10th–14th centuries Arrival of the 'Five Great Clans' in what is now the New Territories.

1557 Portugal establishes official trading colony at Macau.

1699 British East India Company establishes itself in Canton.

1840 First Opium War sparked by a Chinese-imposed ban on the opium trade operated by British and American traders.

1841 British fleet attacks Canton and takes possession of Hong Kong.

1842 Treaty of Nanking: Hong Kong ceded to Britain 'in perpetuity'.

1856–60 The British embark on the Second Opium War, force the opening of further ports and the cession of the Kowloon Peninsula.

1898 Britain negotiates a 99-year lease of the New Territories and the 233 Outlying Islands, until 30 June 1997.

1911 Qing dynasty falls; Sun Yat-sen forms the Republic of China.

1935 Mao Zedong takes control of the Chinese Communist Party.

1941 Hong Kong surrenders to the invading Japanese.

1945 Hong Kong returns to being a British colony.

1950–3 Communist victory on mainland China sees massive waves of refugees swell the local population. Industrialisation commences.

1978 Reforms after the death of Mao Zedong foster increased economic links with China.

1984 Britain signs Joint Declaration for the return of Hong Kong to China.

1997 China resumes sovereignty of Hong Kong.

2003 SARs spreads in Hong Kong, killing 299 people.

2004 Beijing rules out universal suffrage by 2017.

2010 The ICC in Kowloon becomes Hong Kong's tallest building. China's economic success continues to drive Hong Kong's fortunes.

2012 Leung Chun–ying becomes chief executive.

2013 After leaking top-secret national security documents, American Edward Snowden seeks sanctuary in Hong Kong. Total visitor arrivals reach nearly 52.3 million.

WHERE TO GO

The crowded Kowloon peninsula and New Territories on the mainland call for some serious sightseeing, but we begin across Victoria Harbour on Hong Kong Island, where the city was founded and which remains the centre of government, business and commerce.

HONG KONG ISLAND

Central

No matter how many tunnels and transit systems speed up cross-harbour traffic, nothing beats a ride on the **Star Ferry** from Kowloon to **Central District** on Hong Kong Island across Victoria Harbour. As the green-and-white double-decker boats get ready to leave the pier, bells ring, the gangplank is raised and deckhands man the hawsers. On the seven-minute crossing, the ferry weaves its way through an obstacle course of large and small craft, while the soaring skyline of Hong Kong Island draws nearer.

Thanks to land reclamation, the Star Ferry piers are closer together than ever. On 'Hong Kong-side', the Edwardian-style **Central Pier at Pier 7 ❶** was opened in 2006 close to the Airport Express Hong Kong Station and the **International Finance Centre** (IFC, www.

A galaxy of stars

There are 12 boats in the Star Ferry fleet (www.starferry.com.hk), all with different star names: Morning Star, Northern Star, Golden Star, Meridian Star, Day Star, Solar Star, Night Star, Twinkling Star, World Star, Shining Star, Silver Star and Celestial Star. The oldest – Celestial Star – was built in 1956.

The Mid-Levels Escalators

A cluster of architectural landmarks

ifc.com.hk). which includes the Four Seasons Hotel, the IFC Mall and **Two IFC**, at 420m (1,378ft), Hong Kong's second tallest building,

Walkways and footbridges connect all the main buildings in Central. From the IFC, you can walk under cover as far as historic Battery Path in Central, Pacific Place in Admiralty or Western Market in Sheung Wan, or connect with one of Hong Kong's everyday curiosities, the 800m (2,625ft) long outdoor **Central Mid-Levels Escalator** (see page 30).

IFC Mall connects with **Exchange Square ❷**, home to the Hong Kong Stock Exchange. A few minutes east along the walkway is the **General Post Office**, which has philately displays. Across the road is 52-storey **Jardine House**, with porthole-shaped windows, and to the left is an underground walkway that takes you to **Statue Square ❸**. On the east side of the square is one of the few colonial buildings left in the business district, the former Supreme Court (1912).

From Statue Square and **Chater Garden**, look skywards for some contrasting modern architectural landmarks. Most famous is the striking 70-storey I.M. Pei-designed **Bank of China Tower**, not beloved by the people of Hong Kong – its triangular prisms and sharp angles violate the principles of *feng shui* (see opposite) and its radio masts stick up like an insect's antennae. The rival **HSBC Hong Kong headquarters building** is by Norman Foster; built on a 'coathanger frame; its floors hang rather than ascend. From inside the vast atrium you can view the whole structure as well as the mechanical workings of the building. Two bronze lions, Stephen and Sitt (nicknamed for early HSBC Shanghai managers) cast in 1935 guard the entrance, enhancing the bank's *feng shui*.

You can catch one of the historic **trams** along Des Voeux Road and ride from Central to Causeway Bay (see page 37). In 1904 double-decker trams ran along the waterfront, but land reclamation has placed them far inland.

From the HSBC headquarters, cross Queen's Road Central and head up Battery Path to the 1917 French Mission

Feng Shui: seeking prosperity

Feng shui (or *fung shui* in Cantonese) literally means 'wind and water'. An ancient system of divination, its purpose is to achieve harmony with the forces of nature and produce an environment conducive to health and prosperity. Arranging physical premises according to the principles of *feng shui* deflects evil forces and assures the welfare of the inhabitants. Believers moving into a new apartment will call in a *feng shui* geomancer to determine the optimum position of walls, doors and even furniture.

Buildings should face quiet water if possible, or have water nearby, such as a fish tank or a fountain. Lions and dragons are protective. The Hong Kong Bank's doors are guarded by a pair of bronze lions, and the China Resources Building by its Nine Dragons Wall. The famous Bank of China Tower, on the other hand, ignored *feng shui* principles, and is considered an untamed 'dragon's den'.

The dragons of Hong Kong must also receive consideration. New buildings must not block their accustomed pathways to the water, and in one case a new apartment block was constructed with a huge opening in its middle to allow the dragon's passage to the sea.

Building, now the Court Of Final Appeal. Next door is **St John's Cathedral** ❹ (www.stjohnscathedral.org.hk). Built in 1847–9, a mix of neo-Gothic and Norman styles, this Anglican foundation is Hong Kong's oldest and thought to be the oldest in East Asia. It became a club for Japanese officers during World War II. Note the stained-glass windows in the Quiet Chapel, designed by Joseph Edward Nuttgens in the 1950s.

Continue past the cathedral, take the footbridge across Garden Road towards Citibank Plaza and follow signs **for Hong Kong Park** ❺, whose 10.5 hectares (25 acres) of land-scaped gardens and lakes are popular locations for wedding and graduation photos. There's a large **conservatory** with many species of plants plus an excellent raised walk-through **aviary** of birds from Asian rainforests.

In the park is the two-storey **Flagstaff House** (1846), Hong Kong's oldest colonial building, which houses the **Museum of Tea Ware** (Wed–Mon 10am–6pm; free), telling the history of tea from the Warring States period (475–221BC) to the present. Adjacent to the park lies one of Hong Kong's largest and most upmarket shopping malls, **Pacific Place** (www.pacificplace.com.hk). From here, take a 15-minute walk north to see the impressive post-modern **Central Government Complex** ❻ in Tamar on Tim Mei Avenue.

The Peak Tram

Victoria Peak

The most exhilarating way up **Victoria Peak** (552m/ 1,713ft) is by funicular. The **Peak Tram** ❼ (daily

7am–midnight) starts its scenic climb across the street and around the corner from the American Consulate in Garden Road and makes its way, sometimes at a very steep incline, to the upper terminus located at 398m (1,305ft), travelling past fancy apartment blocks, bamboo stands and jungle flowers. Passengers crane their necks for dizzying glimpses of the harbour. The Peak is the most exclusive place to live, reflected in the astronomical property prices and rents. The Peak Tram, originally steam-powered, was built to speed the wealthy *taipans* to their

In St John's Cathedral

mountainside retreats. Before that, sedan chairs and rickshaws were the only way up. Since the tram's inauguration in 1888 it has stopped running only for typhoons and World War II.

The modern 120-passenger cars make the journey in around eight minutes. However, on sunny weekends and public holidays you may have to brave a queue at the lower terminal. The upper terminus opens into the lower levels of **The Peak Tower** ❽ (www.thepeak.com.hk; Mon–Fri 10am–11pm, Sat–Sun 8am–11pm), a distinctive wok-shaped building, packed with shops and plenty of dining options. Entertainment includes interactive games at the EA Experience, a Madame Tussauds wax museum and a magnificent viewing terrace, with a 360-degree panorama of Hong Kong.

Follow the **Peak Circle Walk** along Lugard and Harlech roads for impressive views of Hong Kong, the coastline and the islands in 45 minutes. The view is especially stunning at night. If you're up to a climb, take the **Governor's Walk**, which winds up to the attractive **Victoria Peak Gardens**. They used to belong to the governor's mountain lodge, but the building was demolished by the Japanese during the war.

From the lower terminal of the Peak Tram, it's a short stroll along Upper Albert Road to **Government House**, which was home to 25 of the 28 colonial governors, and is now the official residence of the Chief Executive of the HKSAR, Leung Chun–ying. Across from the mansion, the **Zoological and Botanical Gardens** ❾ (gardens: daily 5am–10pm, zoo: 6am–7pm; free) appeals more for its botany than its animal collections and provides a welcome oasis.

Hollywood Road to Sheung Wan

From 6am to 10am the **Central Mid-Levels Escalator** ferries commuters from the Mid-Levels apartment complexes downhill to Central, then it runs uphill from 10am to midnight, giving a bird's-eye view of street life in Central. The escalator travels above Cochrane Street to Hollywood Road, passing a colourful outdoor 'wet market' along Gage Street and Graham Street, first established here in the 1840s, selling fresh fruit, vegetables, meat and live fish.

The streets around **Hollywood Road** are worth exploring. Pottinger Street (west of Aberdeen, parallel to Cochrane Street), named after Hong Kong's first governor, is known in Chinese as 'stone slab street' for the steps laid down in the 1840s to make it easier for pedestrians and sedan chair bearers to reach Hollywood Road, the second road built in

Graham Street market

the city. Today it is lined with stalls and shops selling haberdashery, clothes and fancy dress outfits and accessories.

Continue up the escalator past Hollywood Road and you'll arrive in **SoHo** with its cosy bars and cafés, trendy restaurants and quirky boutiques. Set lunch menus are excellent value here, while by night it is more laid-back than neighbouring **Lan Kwai Fong** and Wyndham Street or TST's nightlife areas. North of Hollywood Road, NoHo centres around Gough Street's tiny collection of galleries, restaurants, designer homeware and gift shops.

Step off the escalator at Caine Road to find two compact but informative museums. Housed in a restored mansion, the **Dr Sun Yat-sen Museum** ⑩ (http://hk.drsunyatsen. museum; Mon–Wed and Fri 10am–6pm, Sat–Sun 10am–7pm) spells out Hong Kong's role in shaping some of the revolutionary views of the Father of Modern China, who studied medicine in Hong Kong in the late 19th century.

In atmospheric Man Mo Temple

Outside, The Sun Yat-sen Historical Trail marks out 12 significant sites from Sun's time. Many original buildings are gone, but the trail gives an interesting perspective on this fascinating neighbourhood.

A few minutes' walk west along Caine Road is the **Museum of Medical Sciences** ⓫ (www.hkmms. org.hk; Tue–Sat 10am–5pm, Sun 1–5pm; charge). The Edwardian building was formerly the Pathological Institute, founded to combat a 19th-century 30-year outbreak of bubonic plague. The laboratory is still intact and there are interesting exhibits on the development of medical sciences in Hong Kong and the interface between Chinese and Western medicine, plus a herb garden.

Follow Ladder Street down to Hollywood Road, lined with art galleries specialising mainly in contemporary Asian art, and antique shops with an endless collection of Asian ceramics, furniture, carpets, carvings, porcelain and bronze.

Also on Hollywood Road is the **Man Mo Temple** ⓬ (8am–6pm), one of the island's oldest, dating from the 1840s. Visitors are confronted by a dense pall of smoke from the joss sticks and incense coils hanging from the ceiling (these will burn for up to a month). The gold-plated sedan chairs on the left side of the temple were once used for transporting the statues of the temple's gods in religious processions. The statues in the main shrine represent Man Cheong, god of literature, and Mo Tai, god of war and righteousness. Worshippers continue their rituals unperturbed by visitors. To the right of the main hall a fortune teller dispenses advice.

Across the road from the temple, steps on the aptly named Ladder Street lead down to Upper Lascar Row, popularly known as **Cat Street**, for more antiques and curio shops. The nickname apparently refers to the cat burglars who once sold their stolen goods here. Below Cat Street, on Lok Ku Road, junk shops promise hidden vintage treasure.

The border between Central and Sheung Wan is roughly drawn at Aberdeen Street, west of which is one of Hong Kong's oldest neighbourhoods where narrow streets hide a collection of traditional shops. Opposite the Macau Ferry Terminal you'll find **Western Market ⑬**, a former wet market built in 1906, now home to gift shops, a café, and fabric stalls. For an interesting glimpse of small and family-owned shops walk up and down Jervois Street, Bonham Strand, Mercer, Hillier and Cleverly streets. Man Wa Lane is dedicated to craftsmen making traditional Chinese seals or chops, and elsewhere, in between modern grocers, printers, florists and cafés, are old-style tea, noodle and rice merchants, shops selling bamboo steamers and clay-pots for casseroles, or Chinese-style sweets, nuts and snacks, plus an astounding amount of dried seafood, herbs and medicine.

A Cat Street stall

Traditional Chinese medicines

West of Sheung Wan Fong, an open piazza constantly bustling with shoppers and deliveries, the trade in items used in traditional Chinese medicine and cuisine begins to dominate. Wing Lok Street, Bonham Strand West and Ko Shing Street in particular are home to shops trading in birds' nests, dried abalone, dried herbs, roots and fungi, ginseng and, disturbingly, shark's fin. This is the centre of the global trade in shark's fin, claimed as a Chinese delicacy. Once enjoyed by very few, increased affluence has driven demand and many species of shark are now in danger of extinction.

Nearby Possession Street is where the British made their claim on Hong Kong Island in 1841. A short walk along Queen's Road West are what appear to be colourful party decorations shops, with lanterns and buntings, but they also specialise in funeral accessories. Mourners buy paper items to burn for their loved ones – everything from colourful sacks of 'hell' money, so the deceased have some pocket money, to handmade paper models of daily essentials. As well as houses, cars, servants and clothes, today's afterlife accessories include Louis Vuitton luggage, flat-screen televisions and pets.

Take a taxi or any bus heading south (4, 7, 37, 71, 90) up the steep streets to Pok Fu Lam and **Hong Kong University's** campus, which has some original Edwardian buildings. The 1910 foundation stone reveals HKU was established largely with funds from Hormusjee Naorojee Mody, an Indian businessman. The University **Museum and Art Gallery** (94

Bonham Road; www.hkumag.hku.hk; Mon–Sat 9.30am–6pm, Sun 1–6pm; free) holds a significant collection of antiquities: bronzes dating from 3000BC; ceramics including Han Dynasty tomb pottery; and the world's largest collection of Nestorian crosses from the Yuan Dynasty period. At the Tea Gallery, friendly staff explain some of the subtleties of Chinese tea.

Wan Chai

Just to the east of the financial district, **Wan Chai** was once an area of sleazy clubs and topless bars; this was the setting for *The World of Suzie Wong*. Servicemen relaxing from the rigours of the Vietnam War poured millions of dollars into the Wan Chai boom of the 1960s. There is still a rash of

Take a tram

The ancient tram system that travels along Des Voeux, Johnston and Hennessy roads is the most leisurely and revealing way to see Hong Kong. With more than 32km (20 miles) of track, the jerky, electric double-deckers cover almost the entire north coast of the island. Enter at the back of the tram, and try to get a seat in the front of the upper deck for the best views of the colourful streets, always crowded with shoppers and non-stop activity. You'll pass through Wan Chai, where the world of Suzie Wong once existed, and travel all the way to the eastern extremity of Shau Kei Wan. This former pirates' hang-out turned fishing village and shipbuilding centre turned residential area is also home to the Museum of Coastal Defence in the Lei Yue Mun Fort, built in 1887.

The western terminus is in Kennedy Town, a crowded neighbourhood named after a 19th-century Hong Kong governor, Sir Arthur Kennedy. When you're ready to get off the tram, just drop your HK$2 fare in the box at the front beside the driver (www.hktramways.com).

tacky girly clubs here, but also plenty of regular pubs and a smattering of smart cocktail and theme bars.

The Wan Chai waterfront is dominated by the **Hong Kong Convention and Exhibition Centre** ⑭ (HKCEC), which includes a huge exhibition space and two theatres. It hosted the 1997 handover ceremony. Just outside on the Wan Chai promenade the giant **Golden Bauhinia** statue commemorates the establishment of the HKSAR on 1 July 1997 – a must-visit for every mainland tour group. On the other side of Gloucester Road is the **Hong Kong Arts Centre**, with galleries, theatres and an arts cinema, and the **Hong Kong Academy for Performing Arts**, a popular

Typhoon alert

No natural danger poses more of a threat to Hong Kong than a typhoon (*dai fung* or 'big wind' in Cantonese). Typhoons always cause damage, and some disastrous ones have occurred throughout Hong Kong's history. However, although Hong Kong gets around five or more typhoons every year, it is usually spared a direct hit and fatalities are now rare.

Typhoons generally occur between July and September. A series of signals from one to 10 alerts residents in the event of a storm. Signal No. 1 goes up when a tropical storm that could escalate into a typhoon has moved within a 740km (460-mile) radius of Hong Kong. People generally pay little attention at this point. Signal 3 means that the winds have escalated, accompanied, perhaps, by heavy rains. Tours and harbour cruises are suspended, and some businesses close.

No. 8 is more serious: it means that the gale has reached Hong Kong. Banks, offices, museums and most shops and restaurants close, and local transport and flights are disrupted. In case of a No. 8 warning, you should remain in your hotel and check the storm's progress on TV or radio.

venue for visiting international stage shows.

If you follow the tramlines through Wan Chai, you'll find Johnston Road and plenty of factory outlet bargains. At No. 62, a pawnshop and two other century-old shop houses have been beautifully restored and converted into an upmarket restaurant with a pawnshop theme (see page 110). Follow Tai Wong Street or Spring Garden Lane inland to find Wan Chai's street markets.

Hong Kong's harbour from HKCEC

Causeway Bay and beyond

About 2km (1 mile) east of Wan Chai, **Causeway Bay** is second only to Tsim Sha Tsui as *the* place to shop. Packed with malls and department stores, along with several good restaurants, the busy night-and-day crowds make this area vibrant and lively until after midnight.

On the nautical side is the **Causeway Bay Typhoon Shelter**, where expensive yachts are moored, and the Hong Kong Yacht Club has its headquarters. Across Gloucester Road, opposite the World Trade Centre, is the **Noon Day Gun** ⑮, which under British rule was sounded on the stroke of noon. It's not clear how the custom started. One story has it that traders Jardine, Matheson & Co fired a private salute for a visiting tycoon, an act that incensed the colonial authorities, who felt that they had the sole right to issue such a 21-gun welcome. As a result, the merchants were forced to limit their salvoes to one a day – and from then on, they signalled the noon hour daily for all to hear. The gun was made famous by Noel Coward's satirical song *Mad Dogs and Englishmen*. The typhoon shelter will be reclaimed temporarily during the construction of the Central–Wan Chai bypass, but is scheduled to be restored by 2020.

Farther east is Hong Kong's largest park, **Victoria Park** ⑯, with sports grounds, swimming pool and gardens. On the eastern side of the park on Causeway Road is a **Tin Hau Temple**, dedicated to Tin Hau, the Taoist Queen of Heaven and patron of seafarers. Originally the temple was on the shore, but reclamation projects have left it high and dry. On the 23rd day of the Third Moon, the birthday of the goddess is celebrated here and in all Hong Kong fishing communities. In the early morning the park is taken over by people doing t'ai-chi exercises, performing balletic movements in slow motion to discipline the mind and body. On Sunday,

A night at the Happy Valley races

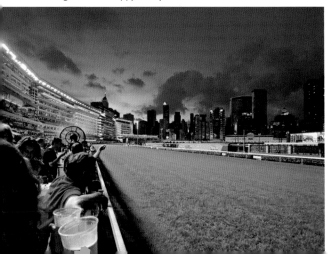

Hong Kong's sizeable community of Indonesian domestic helpers gather here to socialise on their one day off.

At the eastern end of Hong Kong Island, past North Point and Quarry Bay, and best reached on foot (15 minutes) from Shau Kei Wan MTR station, is the **Hong Kong Museum of Coastal Defence** ⑰ (http://hk.coastaldefence.museum; Fri–Wed 10am–5pm; charge). Housed in the restored Lei Yue Mun Fort, built by the British, it showcases 600 years of coastal defence in southern China, from the Ming dynasty to the 1997 handover. A bonus is the hillside location with views across the eastern harbour and plenty of open space and old cannons to explore.

From Shau Kei Wan you can catch a bus or taxi to **Shek O** ⑱, a seaside village with narrow winding streets, a decent beach and some good restaurants. There are great walks into the surrounding hills, and the beach gets packed out on sunny weekends with local families enjoying barbecues. Just round the corner, Shek O's Big Way Bay attracts a smaller crowd of dedicated windsurfers and surfers.

Happy Valley

Inland from Causeway Bay is **Happy Valley** ⑲. At one time this was a very miserable valley, a swamp land conducive only to breeding malarial mosquitoes until it was drained and the horse racing track built in 1873. Now the home of the Hong Kong Jockey Club's racetrack, the stands are packed with punters on Wednesday night from September to July. Except in the members' enclosure, it's a very informal affair; HK$10 gets you into the public stand or track-side beer garden, with inexpensive food and drink, and offers a lively look at Hong Kong life. The **Hong Kong Racing Museum** (www.happyvalleyracecourse.com; Tue–Sun 10am–5pm, race days until 7.30pm; free), provides background information on the sport.

Aberdeen Harbour with the Jumbo Floating Restaurant

Aberdeen

Aberdeen ⑳ is the island's oldest settlement. Once a pirate lair, by the mid-20th century its harbour was home to a large 'floating population' – 'boat people' who spent their entire lives on junks in the harbour, some claiming never to have set foot on land (except for funerals, which weren't thought to count). The majority of the boat people have moved to nearby high-rises but a small community remains. From the Aberdeen promenade, the junks are a picturesque sight: children frolicking on the deck, women preparing food or playing mahjong, dogs and cats underfoot, songbirds in bamboo cages overhead – and all afloat. The boats may appear primitive, but many of them have electric generators and all modern conveniences. You can tour the port in one of the small *sampan* – around HK$80 for a half-hour tour (pay at the end and negotiate a discount for two or more people).

Aberdeen's delightfully gaudy Jumbo Floating Restaurant, revamped and rebranded as **Jumbo Kingdom**, has featured in many a movie. It is well worth boarding the free shuttle (Mon–Sat 11am–11.30pm, Sun 9am–11.30pm) across the harbour to explore and eat. There's a seafood exhibition, a Chinese restaurant and the excellent Top Deck with alfresco international cuisine, seafood and great views.

Ocean Park

Ocean Park ㉑ (www.oceanpark.com.hk; 10am–7.30pm; charge; book in advance for behind-the-scenes tours) is Hong Kong's home-grown theme park, with almost 70 attractions, including scary rides and roller-coasters, and an oceanarium with dolphins, sea lions, seals and penguins. It is divided into two areas: The Summit and The Waterfront, linked by a cable car that offers spectacular views. The top attractions among its Amazing Asian Animals are two pairs of bamboo-munching pandas: An An and Jia Jia, and youngsters Le Le and Ying Ying. The atoll reef with layers of sea life, the shark tunnel and eerie jellyfish displays are also crowd pleasers.

Repulse Bay

Continuing around the coast in a counter-clockwise direction, Deep Water Bay offers a good beach and harbours. The next inlet is **Repulse Bay ㉒**, a sandy crescent backed by green hills and busy with day-trippers. Notice the massive wall of condominiums, built in the 1980s. Apparently the developers left the space in the middle for good *feng shui* – to enable the mountain's 'dragon spirit' to retain access to the sea.

Stanley

Stanley ㉓ was once one of the main fishing villages on the island. **Stanley Market** (www.hk-stanley-market.com;

A stroll along the Waterfront Promenade should be done at least twice during any stay in Hong Kong, once by day and once by night. And if you're in Hong Kong for Chinese New Year, this is the place to be to see the fireworks bursting across the city, but stake your position early for a good view.

10am–6pm) is well known for its clothes bargains in 'Western sizes' – plus plenty of souvenirs. The waterfront is lined with restaurants and bars, many of them with sea-view balconies. A few minutes' walk along the bay are **Stanley Plaza** shopping mall and historic **Murray House**. The latter, built in Central in 1844, dismantled in 1982, and rebuilt here in 1999, houses the **Hong Kong Maritime Museum** (www.hkmaritimemuseum.org; Tue–Fri and Sun 10am–6pm, Sat 10am–7pm; charge) which tells the story of shipping in Hong Kong.

KOWLOON

Though much smaller than Hong Kong Island, Kowloon has almost twice the population. In many areas, the density reaches 150,000 inhabitants per sq kilometre (0.25 sq mile). Most of the area's attractions are centred near the tip of the peninsula in the **Tsim Sha Tsui** district. Next to the Star Ferry terminal is **Ocean Terminal**, where international cruise ships dock; and **Harbour City**. Five minutes along Austin Road on the west side of Tsim Sha Tsui a large reclamation project is home to the Airport Express and MTR's Kowloon Station, Elements Mall and the **International Commerce Centre (ICC)** ❷, which at 484m (1,588ft) is Hong Kong's tallest building. The viewing platform on the 100th floor and Sky Dining 101 on the 101th (www.shkp.icc.com) give exceptional views of the city.

Waterfront

From the Star Ferry terminal, amid the malls and pink-tiled government buildings, two historical buildings stand out. **Hullett House** is the former Marine Police headquarters built in 1883 to overlook the comings and goings in the harbour. Now a boutique hotel, it can be explored by joining daily tours, or by visiting its restaurants and bars. Less pleasingly, but very much in Hong Kong's money-making tradition, the hillock the police station was built on has been carved out and converted into a faux Victorian shopping arcade – **1881 Heritage**.

At the start of the **Tsim Sha Tsui Waterfront Promenade**, the 1910 **Clock Tower** ❷⑤ is all that remains of the once grand Kowloon–Canton Railway Terminus, where trains used to depart from Hong Kong for Paris. The promenade offers unparalled views of the harbour and

Tsim Sha Tsui's Clock Tower

The Avenue of the Stars, with a view across to Central

Hong Kong Island. The Avenue of Stars (www.avenueof stars.com.hk), Hong Kong's version of the Hollywood Walk of Fame, is here – a star-studded path that honours those involved in the territory's film industry. Few of the names will be familiar, but you will recognise Bruce Lee, Chow Yun Fat and Jackie Chan.

Flanked by the clock tower is the imposing **Hong Kong Cultural Centre** 26. The major venue for the performing arts, it has been criticised for its fortress-like architecture and windowless facade on a site with one of the most magnificent views in the world. The interior is a comfortable amalgam of Chinese and Western design, with an impressive main lobby. There are two concert halls and a studio theatre.

Museums

Next is the **Hong Kong Space Museum** (http://hk.space. museum; Mon, Wed–Fri 1–9pm, Sat–Sun 10am–9pm;

charge). Its futuristic dome design is striking; inside are interactive exhibits, including one in which you can experience weightlessness. The theatre (charge) presents 'sky shows' and IMAX films.

The **Hong Kong Museum of Art** (http://hk.art.museum; Mon–Wed and Fri 10am–6pm, Sat–Sun 10am–7pm; charge) stands behind the Space Museum. Permanent collections include: the Xubaizhi collection of painting, calligraphy, ceramics and antiquities; contemporary Hong Kong art; and historical collections of paintings of the region.

A few blocks up Chatham Road South are two more museums. The **Hong Kong Science Museum** (http://hk.science.museum; Mon–Wed, Fri 1–7pm, Sat–Sun 10am–9pm; charge) is a state-of-the-art interactive museum that will teach you how everything works, from ancient sailing ships to the latest technology. If you only have time for one museum, choose the excellent **Hong Kong Museum of History** ㉗ (http://hk.history.museum; Mon, Wed–Fri 10am–6pm, Sat–Sun until 7pm; charge). It tells The Hong Kong Story in eight galleries, using a variety of media to cover the natural environment, prehistoric finds and folk culture, as well as Hong Kong's development as a metropolis over the last 170-plus years. Painful episodes such as the Opium Wars and the Japanese occupation are covered, as is the back story to Hong Kong's remarkable economic success. Short videos tell the story of each gallery, in English, Cantonese and Putonghua.

Peninsula Hotel

Located just across Salisbury Road from the cultural centre is the historic hotel, **The Peninsula Hong Kong**, expanded and modernised by a 32-storey tower. Opened in 1928, The Peninsula was the first hotel on Kowloon, strategically positioned for passengers arriving overland from China and

Trinkets at the Jade Market

Europe by train. The lobby became a favourite rendezvous for high society, and guests still sit beneath the restored gilt stucco ceiling to see and be seen. High tea or cocktails to the strains of the resident string orchestra are a wonderful way to recapture the atmosphere of a bygone age.

Nathan Road

Alongside the hotel runs busy **Nathan Road**, Hong Kong's fabled shopping street, lined with shops, hotels and restaurants. Kowloon's main street was created by Sir Matthew Nathan when he was governor of Hong Kong at the turn of the 19th century. When it was constructed, many thought it absurd to have a tree-lined boulevard running through what was practically wilderness. First known as 'Nathan's Folly', later as the 'Golden Mile', Nathan Road's retail options range from the latest fashions in iSquare mall or the Miramar Shopping Centre and iconic neon-signed electronics shops to discount cosmetic stores and the infamous **Chungking Mansions**, famous for its cheap guesthouses and authentic Indian restaurants; uniquely, it is distinctly neither Western nor Chinese in character.

A few blocks up the road is elegant **Kowloon Park** ❷❽ (daily 5am–midnight), with fountains, promenades and ornamental gardens; go up the steps to the Sculpture Walk, where artists from Hong Kong and elsewhere exhibit their works.

The **Hong Kong Heritage Discovery Centre** (Mon–Wed and Fri 10am–6pm, Sat–Sun 10am–7pm; free) was built around 1910 as barracks for the colonial police force; now it houses occasional exhibitions and offers some cool respite from Kowloon crowds. The mosque in the southeast corner of the park is the largest in the territory with four minarets. Hong Kong has around 80,000 Muslims.

Further up Nathan Street is **Yau Ma Tei**, one of the older parts of Kowloon. Take a left turn off Nathan and walk down Kansu to the **Jade Market** ❷❾ (9am–6pm), with more than 100 stalls spread out in a tent, just before the overpass.

Temple Street Night Market

Hong Kong's liveliest market is the **Temple Street Night Market** ❸⓿ (4pm–midnight), near Jordan Road. Everything is sold here, from clothing to souvenirs to electronic goods, and bargaining is an intrinsic part of the experience. Pause to enjoy a dish or two straight from the wok at one of the food stalls that spread out along the

Exploring Kowloon

KMB Bus 11 (www.kmb.hk) crosses Kowloon from Diamond Hill to Kowloon MTR station. It stops at Wong Tai Sin and Kowloon Walled City Park, and passes close to the Thai restaurants on the streets around Nga Tsin Wai Road.

In the Bird Garden

pavements each night. The market runs all the way to **Tin Hau Temple**, where you will find fortune tellers (some speak English) and possibly street performers singing Chinese opera (or pop songs). The temple is one of many dedicated to Tin Hau, goddess of seafarers; it also houses an altar to Shing Wong, the city's god.

Mong Kok

The markets are what draws most visitors to Mong Kok. The **Ladies' Market** (www.ladies-market.hk; daily noon–10.30pm), on Tung Choi Street has stalls selling cheap T-shirts, jeans, watches and souvenirs, plus handbags and lingerie, which seems to justify the market's name. Between Argyle Street and Mong Kok Road, Tung Choi becomes the **Goldfish Market** (daily 10am–6pm), specialising in everything that could possibly be needed to keep fish in aquariums. The parallel section of Fa Yuen Street is lined with factory outlets.

Further north past Prince Edward Road West the daily **Flower Market** (www.flower-market.hk; 7am–7pm) is a visual treat, with an array of tropical flowers including an amazing selection of orchids. At the far end you'll find the Yuen Po Street **Bird Garden** ③ (www.bird-garden.hk; daily 7am–6pm). Songbirds are highly prized by their owners, who take them for walks, carrying the bamboo or wooden cages through the streets. The birds entertain passers-by with a symphony of shrill arias; you will also find traditional cages for sale.

Further north in Sham Shui Po, west of the junction of Nathan Road and Boundary Street, is the **Lei Cheng Uk Han Tomb and Museum** ❷ (Mon–Wed, Fri–Sun 10am–6pm) on Tonkin Street. This ancient burial vault is believed to date back to the Han Dynasty (ad25–220). The barrel-vaulted chambers were discovered during excavations in 1955 for a government housing project (Cheung Sha Wan MTR, Bus 2 from Star Ferry TST).

Wong Tai Sin

One of Hong Kong's brightest, biggest and busiest temples is the Sik Sik Yuen **Wong Tai Sin Temple** ❸ (www.siksik yuen.org.hk; daily 7am–5.30pm; Wong Tai Sin MTR) in northeast Kowloon. It is dedicated to a shepherd boy from Zhejiang who had special healing powers and came to be revered as a demi-god after his death. The incense-wreathed

Chi Lin Nunnery

Nian Lin Garden pavilion

temple complex, which has halls dedicated to the Taoist, Confucian and Buddhist faiths, is especially packed at Lunar New Year as people come here to pray for prosperity and to rattle fortune sticks. The temple has given its name to a densely populated district, home to 440,000 people, that comprised villages until the influx of refugees in the late 1940s. Dominated by squatter villages in the 1950s and 1960s, it was transformed by huge government housing estates.

At nearby Diamond Hill (MTR), the **Chi Lin Nunnery** ❹ (daily, halls: 9am–4.30pm, garden: 7am–7pm) established on a remote hillside in the 1930s has been surrounded by high-rise towers and development as historical forces transformed the area. Rebuilt completely in wood during the 1990s in the style of a Tang Dynasty timber monastery, with classic flying eaves, the complex demonstrates an elegant aesthetic throughout. Surrounded by lotus ponds, its many halls are home to remarkable golden statues of Buddhist deities and the Sakyamuni Buddha.

Across the road, the **Nian Lin Garden** (daily 7am–9pm; free) is one of the most beautiful Chinese gardens in Hong Kong. Also following Tang aesthetics, the garden features classic ornamental rocks, pavilions and water features plus a collection of beautifully shaped rare trees. A vegetarian restaurant, with a convenient location behind the waterfall, is a unique venue for Chinese Buddhist fare.

Kowloon Walled City

South of Wong Tai Sin and Diamond Hill is another attractive garden, built to commemorate the notorious Kowloon Walled City, which remained Chinese territory after the British leased the New Territories in 1898. A haven for illegal activity, the ramshackle multi-storey slum was demolished in 1992.

Kowloon Walled City Park ③⑤ (daily 6.30am–11pm) is modelled on a Jiangen garden from the early Qing dynasty and has preserved the southern gate of the old walled city.

The New Territories can be explored via buses and the MTR network, including an overland Light Rail Transit (LRT) system connecting towns and estates in the west. Route maps at stops and stations are bilingual and the Octopus card makes it simple. Green New Territories taxis are also an option. The HKTB's Land Between and Heritage tours are good ways to cover a lot of ground in a short time.

Tsuen Wan

Tsuen Wan is typical of the pattern of development of the New Territories and was the first new town to be developed in the 1960s to deal with desperate overcrowding in Kowloon and Hong Kong. Northwest of Kowloon, at the end of an MTR line, this was a rice-farming area with a small market a century ago, it is now home to 305,600.

Set amid Tsuen Wan's residential towers, a short walk from the MTR station, is the 18th-century walled village of **Sam Tung Uk** ③⑥. Built by a Chan clan in 1786, it is preserved as a museum (Wed–Mon 9am–6pm; free), displaying period furniture and farming implements, as well

Strolling in Hong Kong Wetland Park

as exhibitions on Chinese folk culture. The displays offer an excellent perspective on life in a walled village and the changes in the area.

The journey from Tsuen Wan to Tuen Mun takes 30–45 minutes by road and the 66M bus from Tsuen Wan bus station gives great views of the coast and the Tsing Kau and Tsing Ma Bridges as it winds along the coast. A third of all Hong Kong's beaches are found in a single 14km (9-mile) stretch of this region's shoreline. Place names are often based on the distance to the nearest mile-post, as measured from the tip of the Kowloon peninsula. Thus you find '19.5 mile Beach' at Castle Peak Bay. To the northeast, with a great view over the New Territories and Guangdong, is Hong Kong's highest peak, **Tai Mo Shan** (57m/3,140ft).

In **Tuen Mun**, surrounded by the Tai Hing Estate (beside the Ching Chung Koon LRT station, look out for bamboo-lined fencing, colourful rooftops and arches), is the Taoist retreat of **Ching Chung Koon** ㊲, which warrants a visit if you are in the vicinity. This 'Temple of Green Pines' is a colouful complex containing temples and pavilions and bonsai. Apart from making a brief appearance in the opening scene of Bruce Lee's *Enter the Dragon*, Ching Chung Koon is a home for the elderly and has memorial halls where ancestors' remains are stored in tiny niches bearing photos, and respects are paid daily.

Hong Kong Wetland Park

On the Light Rail system, with its own station, **Hong Kong Wetland Park** ㊳ (www.wetlandpark.gov.hk; Wed–Mon 10am–5pm) covers an area of 61 hectares (151 acres), and shows the diversity of Hong Kong's wetland ecosystem. The park is between the high rises of Tin Shui Wai and Shenzhen across the border. Circular walks meander through the wetlands and there are hides with telescopes for birdwatching. Almost 130 bird species have been recorded here, including varieties of egret and heron, and the rare black-faced

Wild and beautiful

Remote areas of the New Territories and sections of Lantau Island are happy sighting grounds for birdwatchers. Hundreds of species have been recorded, from everyday egrets and funny-faced cockatoos to mynahs and pelicans. The Sai Kung Peninsula Nature Preserve has many hiking trails for the nature lover.

As civilisation encroaches, wild animals and their habitats are threatened, but there are a few thousand monkeys living in the hills around the Kowloon reservoir and you still come across barking deer, wild pigs, porcupines, civets and scaly anteaters. In the wilderness you may also stumble upon a banded krait, a cobra, or some other fearsome snake. Though sightings are common, bitings are rare.

Hakka woman at
Kat Hing Wai

spoonbill. Numerous buses, including bus 967 from Admiralty via Central and West Kowloon, stop at the Wetland Park entrance.

Ping Shan Heritage Trail

Two stops along the LRT, Tin Shui Wah stop is the start of the **Ping Shan Heritage Trail** ❸⁹, a 1km (0.6-mile) walk through villages where sites include the 600-year-old Tsui Sing Lau Pagoda, a walled village, shrines, temples, study halls and the ancestral hall of the Tang clan, one of the Five Great Clans that migrated here from North China. The well-signed trail includes a five-minute hike up a small hill where a 1899 police station has been cleverly converted into the **Ping Shan Tang Clan Gallery** (daily 10am–5pm), with displays of village life and old photographs. The trail ends conveniently close to the Ping Shan Light Rail station.

Kam Tin and Lo Wai

Kat Hing Wai ❹⁰, one of the most easily accessible of the New Territories' walled villages, is located in the village of Kam Tin at Kan Sheun Road MTR station. The huge new station is set in an open plain surrounded by imposing mountains, and hosts an outdoor market selling household items, gifts, toys and plants each weekend. A 10-minute walk over a bridge and past an indoor market (with stalls selling decorative items, water features, paintings, wine and plants), takes you through narrow alleys to the walled village, which is surrounded by the remains of a stagnant moat and a sprawling modern village.

Kat Hing Wai village is built in a square, and the only way in is through a gate in the defensive wall, now guarded by senior village ladies clad in traditional black Hakka garments, wearing functional Hakka bamboo hats, with black fringes that provide excellent protection from both sun and tropical rain. Kat Hing Wai was built four or five centuries ago, also by the Tang clan. Many of the old houses inside the walled village have been replaced by modern structures.

The Tang clan's earliest walled village was **Lo Wai**, northeast of Fanling (MTR), which also has its defensive wall intact. Adjacent to the village is the restored **Tang Chung Ling Ancestral Hall** ➍ (open Wed–Mon 9am–1pm and 2–5pm), which dates from the early 16th century. Few traditional ancestral halls remain in China since the Cultural

Day-trip to Shenzhen

Just over the Guangdong border, Shenzhen was China's first Special Economic Zone, set up in the 1970s as the answer to Hong Kong. It has grown into a metropolis of more than 10 million people, with tightly clustered skyscrapers and some of China's highest grossing industries.

Shenzhen's main tourist attractions are its enormous theme parks. One of them, **Splendid China** (daily 9am–6pm), purports to show 'all of China in one day'. At the weekend some Hong Kong residents head to Shenzhen for cheaper golf, dining and entertainment, while shoppers visit primarily for the **Lo Wu Commercial Centre**, with its 1,500 shops. Shenzhen is very easy to reach – the MTR trains run all day (about 40 minutes from Hung Hom station). Visitors need a China visa and must disembark at Lo Wu, the Hong Kong/Guangdong border checkpoint.

Pagoda at the Monastery of 10,000 Buddhas

Revolution, so these New Territories ancestral halls are rare survivors. Another such hall, belonging to the Liu Clan, is **Liu Man Shek Tong** ㊷ in the village of Sheung Shui, and is a 15-minute walk from the MTR station.

Kadoorie Farm and Botanic Garden

A trip to **Kadoorie Farm and Botanic Garden** ㊸ (www.kfbg.org.hk; daily 9.30am–5pm) is highly recommended. Reached by taxi or the 64K bus heading east from Kan Sheun Road MTR, or heading west from Tai Wo MTR station, the farm sits in the middle of the New Territories at the foot of Tai Mo Shan. KFBG was founded by the Kadoorie family in 1951 to provide support for immigrant farmers from the Chinese mainland. It is best known as a centre for conserving plants and indigenous animals as well as conducting research into sustainable agriculture.

Visitors can explore the greenhouses, the insect and reptile houses, the Wild Animal Rescue Centre, ecology projects and follow nature trails along or up the slopes of the farm. The upper peak of the garden is named Kwun Yum Shan (552m/1,800ft) and a stroll up there takes about two hours to complete.

Sha Tin

Beyond Wong Tai Sin, on the northeast side of the New Territories, lies **Sha Tin** District. Two thirds of its population of 647,000 live in government subsidised housing and there arc 30,000 people living in villages, crammed on slopes around the urban suburbs. Sha Tin is a good stopping point before or after venturing into the New Territories countryside. Its biggest attraction is the **Monastery of 10,000 Buddhas ⑭**, also known as **Man Fat Tze**, set on a hillside above the main Sha Tin New Town. Follow the signposts from Sha Tin MTR Station, along Pai Tau Street to the start of a 500-step climb to the monastery.

Regiments of small gilt statues of Buddha (12,800 of them) line the walls of the altar room. The monastery was founded in 1957 by Yuet Kai, who died in 1965 at the age of 87. He had predicted that his body would not decompose if he were buried behind the temple in a crouching position. True enough, when his body was exhumed eight months later, it was still in good condition. His corpse was covered in gold leaf and placed in a building on the second level. You can climb to the top of the nine-storey pagoda for panoramic views.

Seafood selection at Sai Kung

From the monastery you can see Lion's Rock (495m/ 1,600ft), shaped like a lion lying in wait, a small rock formation known as **Amah (Mother) Rock**, which is actually a pile of several rocks that resemble a woman with a baby in a sling on her back. Legend has it that a local woman climbed the

hill every day to watch for her husband returning from across the sea; one day the wife and her child were turned to stone as a permanent symbol of her enduring faith. **Lion Rock Country Park ㊺**, the 5.57 sq km (2 sq miles) of forested hills between Sha Tin and Kowloon can be explored by hiking along either stage 5 of the Maclehose Trail or stage 5 of the slightly easier Wilson Trail.

Also in Sha Tin, by the Shing Mun River Channel, is the **Hong Kong Heritage Museum ㊻** (www.heritage museum.gov.hk; Mon, Wed–Fri 10am–6pm, Sat–Sun 10am–7pm; charge). The museum contains a fun interactive guide to Cantonese opera, art galleries and exhibits dedicated to telling the story of Hong Kong's culture and history.

Down to earth, the **Sha Tin Racecourse** can accommodate more than 80,000 spectators and is equipped with every imaginable luxury, including a giant video screen

A picturesque bay on the Sai Kung peninsula

facing the stands, and air-conditioned stables for the horses. Opposite the Sha Tin railway station, **New Town Plaza** features shops, cinemas and even a computer-controlled musical fountain.

At University station is the campus of the **Chinese University of Hong Kong**. The **Art Museum** (Mon–Wed and Fri–Sat 10am–5pm, Sun 1–5pm; free) in the Institute of Chinese Studies is worth a visit for its painting and calligraphy collections.

> **Getting to Lantau**
>
> Lantau can be reached by road and MTR, as well as by ferry. Visitors to Disneyland can take the special MTR Disneyland Resort line, which runs 3.5km (2 miles) between Sunny Bay and the Disneyland terminus, aboard special Disney-themed trains.

Sai Kung

The scenic **Sai Kung Peninsula** ❹ lies to the east of Sha Tin. It takes about 40–60 minutes to reach Sai Kung town by bus 94 from Diamond Hill MTR station, or by green taxi. At the end of the journey, there is a pretty seaside village to explore with plenty of seafood restaurants and options for alfresco dining, as well as two public piers busy with boats and junks setting off for outings around the craggy coastline and islands.

From the nearby ferry pier you can catch a boat to **Kau Sai Chau**, an island with a public golf course. **Tap Mun** is a more remote island, but can be reached via the 94 bus and ferry from Wong Shek Pier; though barely populated, it has a seafood restaurant.

Staying on the peninsula, the Jockey Club **Wong Shek Water Sports Centre** hires out kayaks, windsurfboards and dinghies if you are appropriately qualified, and there are two easy family trails that allow you to take in the scenery.

OUTLYING ISLANDS

Around Hong Kong there are more than 235 outlying islands. Many are uninhabited or home to very small communities. The major islands of Lantau, Cheung Chau and Lamma are full of fascinating contrasts and it is worth setting aside a couple of half days to visit. Start your exploration at the Outlying Islands Ferry Piers in front of the IFC, and catch one of the cheap and reasonably comfortable ferries used by the islanders. For ferry information, see page 126.

Lantau

Ferries depart from Central Pier 6 at least every hour from 6.10am until late at night to **Mui Wo (Silvermine Bay)**, where you can catch buses to all parts of the island.

Most of Lantau is still remarkably tranquil despite additions such as Hong Kong International Airport, which opened in 1996 at Chek Lap Kok on the northwest coast. At the same time, a huge new town was built nearby at Tung Chung, and the Tsing Ma road-rail bridge connected Lantau to the New Territories. Hong Kong Disneyland Resort has also brought millions more visitors. Yet much of it remains rural, with more than half of it protected parkland. There is a 69km (43-mile) circular hiking trail (see page 92). At 934m (3,064ft), **Lantau Peak** is high enough to attract the occasional rain cloud – cool breezes blow on most hot days.

Leaving an offering at Po Lin Monastery

The giant Tian Tan Buddha

Visitors intending to include a beach in their itinerary should head for beautiful **Cheung Sha Beach**, by bus (No. 2) or taxi from Mui Wo. At 3km (2 miles) long it's one of the longest in Hong Kong and has flat white sands and a couple of good restaurants.

Lantau's most famous site is the world's tallest seated bronze statue of Buddha, the 22m (73ft) **Tian Tan Buddha** ❽. The 'Big Buddha' can be reached by bus from Mui Wo (No. 2) or if the weather is calm and fine, the Ngong Ping 360 cable car (www.np360.com.hk; Mon–Fri 10am–6pm, Sat–Sun 9am–6.30pm), can be boarded near Tung Chung MTR and bus station for breathtaking views over Lantau. On clear days, views on the 25-minute journey across Lantau are dramatic, and the fearless can travel in a cabin with a glass floor. The journey ends at the beautiful village of **Ngong Ping**, with new but attractive Ming Dynasty-style buildings, Chinese teashops and two multimedia theatres

Relaxing in Cheung Chau

telling the story of Buddha. If you want to escape the crowds, follow the Wisdom Trail around Ngong Ping or the steep trail to Lantau Peak (934m/3,064ft), Hong Kong's second-highest mountain.

Nearby is **Po Lin Monastery** (www.plm.org.hk; daily 8am–6pm, vegetarian lunch: 11.30am–4.30pm) and the rewarding walk up 268 steps to the Tian Tan Buddha statue and glorious views. The monastery is strictly vegetarian and visitors are warned not to bring any meat with them.

From Ngong Ping you can travel by land for an hour through hills dotted with more remote monasteries, by taxi or bus (21) to the pretty fishing village at **Tai O** ㊾. The Kwan Tai temple dates from 1530. Many villagers are descended from Tanka fishing people and live in stilt houses above the water. Tai O is a good place to try to spot Hong Kong's endangered pink dolphin from land, but from the water only organised tours such as Dolphinwatch (see page 120) are sanctioned by conservationists. The village is also home to the Hong Kong Shaolin Wushu Centre (www.shaolincc.org.hk), which promotes the traditional Chinese martial art. Take bus 11 back to Tung Chung MTR or bus 1 back to Ngong Ping.

Lantau's mountains provide a stunning backdrop to **Hong Kong Disneyland** ㊿ (www.hongkongdisneyland.com; daily, park hours, show and firework display times change regularly). There are two hotels: Disney's Hollywood Hotel and the Victorian-style Hong Kong Disneyland Hotel, which also offer good views of Hong Kong and up-close views of the nightly fireworks, as well as extending the Disneyland experience. The resort's attractions and layout are similar to other locations in Paris, Tokyo and the US, but the park is smaller, which can be more attractive if you are travelling with younger children or have limited time. It is divided into different themed areas: the nostalgic Main Street; Fantasyland, set around a fairytale castle; Adventureland featuring the Jungle River Cruise and Tarzan's Treehouse; and Tomorrowland focusing on space exploration, featuring a dramatic roller-coaster and other extraterrestrial thrills.

Cheung Chau

Some 10km (6 miles) west of Hong Kong lies the small, crowded island of **Cheung Chau** ⑤ (around 2.5 sq km/1

Tai O Village

Bun Festival activities

sq mile in size). More than 25,000 people live here, many of them fishermen, but there is also an expat community, attracted by the laid-back Mediterranean ambience. The island has a checkered past of smuggling and piracy.

Cheung Chau becomes the centre of Hong Kong life once a year, usually in May, during the **Bun Festival**, a folklore extravaganza. For the rest of the year, life goes on at its accustomed pace: rickety machines chugging in two-man factories, children in school uniforms being ferried home to houseboats and elderly fishermen stirring shrimp paste.

By way of formal attractions, **Pak Tai Temple**, built in 1783, has some fine carvings and a great iron sword said to be 600 years old. Pak Tai means 'Ruler of the North' and he is usually represented in a sitting position, with his feet resting on a tortoise and a snake. The statue is credited with saving the village from a plague in the 18th century.

From the main township of **Cheung Chau** it's possible to walk via the harbour road (15 minutes) or the scenic Peak Road (45 minutes) to the village of **San Wai**, which has a temple dedicated to Tin Hau, goddess of the sea and protectress of fisherfolk. You can also take a *kai do*, or water taxi from the pier next to the ferry pier.

The **Praya**, the promenade in front of the ferry pier, is a good place to observe the junks and fishing boats in the harbour. There are also several open-air restaurants where you can enjoy fresh seafood. At the other side of the island, at the end of Tung Wan Road, is the popular **Tung Wan Beach**. Further along the headland is Kwun Yam Wan beach, where you can hire boards from the windsurfing centre.

Lamma

Less than 30 minutes by ferry from Pier 4 in Central, **Lamma Island** ❷ is perfect for hiking, picnicking, bird-watching, lazing on the beach or just relaxing and exploring

Getting to and around Macau

The easiest way to get to Macau is by TurboJET ferry (www.turbojet. com.hk). Jetfoils run every 15 to 30 minutes, 24 hours a day from the Macau Ferry Terminal at the Shun Tak Centre in Sheung Wan, just west of the Central ferry piers. The trip to Macau's main ferry terminal takes about an hour. There are also four departures daily from the Sky Pier near the Hong Kong International Airport (45 minutes).

Cotai Jet Ferries (www.cotaiwaterjet.com) run services between 7am and 5pm from the Shun Tak Centre to a new pier in Macau on Taipa.

The Macau Government Tourist Office at 336–7 Shun Tak Centre (www.macautourism.gov.mo) can assist with information. Most nationalities need only a passport to enter Macau. The *pataca*, Macau's currency, is pegged to the Hong Kong dollar, and you can use Hong Kong currency in Macau.

There is another Macau Government Tourist Office at the main ferry teminal in Macau. Outside, there are free shuttle buses to hotels and casinos, as well as taxis and minibuses to all points (take 3, 3A, 10, or 10A to the historic centre; exact change required).

St Paul's Baroque facade

a car-free village at your own pace. Hong Kong's third largest island has a population of only about 6,000; it is still largely undeveloped and has a very laid-back atmosphere. Archaeologists believe that Lamma has probably been inhabited for some 4,000 years, and relics from 'Hong Kong's Stone Age Island' are on display at the Hong Kong Museum of History. The largest structure on the island is the gigantic power station that supplies electricity to the whole of Hong Kong Island.

Try and plan a trip for a weekday if you can, as Lamma tends to be swamped by day-trippers at the weekend and on public holidays. You will need to visit in May and June to see the Dragonboat and Tin Hau festivals.

Lamma's principal settlements are **Yung Shue Wan** on the northwest coast and **Sok Kwu Wan** to the south. Both villages have ferry services and waterfront restaurants with excellent and inexpensive Cantonese food, and plenty of fresh seafood.

Most of the population is Chinese, but Yung Shue Wan is an unusually multicultural enclave.

EXCURSION TO MACAU

Macau, the final bastion of Portugal's great 16th-century empire, is much more than just a quirk of history. Here,

Shopping and dining in Macau

Shopping: Like Hong Kong, Macau is a duty-free port. Shops aimed at the tourist market are interspersed with the more workaday ironmongers, herbalists and noodle stalls. Knowledgeable visitors look for antiques – either Chinese heirlooms or remnants from the Portuguese colonial days. Both antiques and excellent reproductions of 18th- and 19th-century Chinese furniture are found on Rua de São Paolo. Wynn Macau has an arcade packed with international brand names, and at The Venetian Macao you can explore The Grand Canal Shoppes by gondola. Also worth exploring are the Sunday market at Taipa and the small antique and reproduction furniture shops in Coloane.

Dining: Macau's own cuisine is a combination of Chinese cooking styles and ingredients, infused with flavours imported from Portugal, Brazil and Africa. Whether you choose to eat in one of the Chinese, traditional Portuguese or international-style restaurants, you will get a hearty meal at a good price. African chicken with fries is a Macau favourite. Portuguese egg tarts and pork chop buns are popular Macanese snacks.

Fresh fish and seafood is particularly good. A delicate, delicious fish is Macau sole (*linguado*). Imported dried cod (*bacalhao*) is the Portuguese national dish; several varieties are available, usually baked. Macau has an ample supply of Portuguese wines. Try *vinho verde*, a mildly sparkling young wine from northern Portugal, or a hearty red Dão or Colares. After dinner, a glass of Madeira or port is recommended.

Traditional custard tarts at Lord Stow's Bakery

where East and West first met, parts of the enclave still beautifully combine a taste of Asia with something of the sunny atmosphere of the Mediterranean. In its 21st-century incarnation, Macau has also taken on some of the exuberance of Las Vegas, thanks to the excitement that the new casino developments and booming visitor numbers have generated.

Macau's historic centre, the Largo do Senado, with its colonial architecture, has a distinctly Mediterranean flavour. Colonnaded public buildings, iron balconies, winding streets, flagstoned squares and many churches all speak of the Portuguese inheritance as well as the Chinese, a fusion of East and West that has produced the unique Macanese culture.

The story of the European discovery of Macau begins in 1513, when Portuguese explorer Jorge Alvares reached the south coast of China. Traders followed in his wake, setting up bases in several parts of the Pearl River estuary. Finally, in 1557, they were all consolidated in Macau. It was the only European gateway to China, and through it flowed Western technology and religion. In 1576, Pope Gregory XIII created the Macau diocese, which covered all of China and Japan.

The location presented significant trade opportunities. As China and Japan were not on speaking terms, trade between them had to be channelled through a neutral middleman and Macau was ideal. Portugal's resulting near-monopoly of East–West trade awakened the competitive instincts of other European powers. The Dutch sent an invasion flotilla to Macau in 1622, but the defenders triumphed. However, the end of the golden age was drawing near. China began to relax trade restrictions, and with the rise of Hong Kong, Macau became an isolated Portuguese outpost.

In the 17th century Macau provided a haven for persecuted Japanese Christians, and during World War II Portugal's neutrality brought the territory a new flood of refugees. They were joined by a swarm of spies of all conceivable nationalities, and Macau won a name for international intrigue.

The territory was formally handed back to China in 1999. Now known as the Macau Special Administrative Region (MSAR), it is governed under a 'one country, two systems' set-up, similar to that in Hong Kong.

In recent years the region's landscape has changed significantly, primarily as a result of the opening up of the MSAR's gaming industry. Ambitious reclamation has created new land (known as the NAPE zone) on the Macau peninsula's Porto Exterior (Outer Harbour) and, most dramatically, the islands of Coloane and Taipa have been joined by reclaimed land called Cotai. Macau is the only place in Greater China where gaming

Historic route

To explore the 25 buildings that make up the Unesco Historic Centre of Macau, follow the route from Largo Senado to the A-Ma Temple or vice versa. Maps are available at the Macau Tourism offices at the ferry terminals Either way is rewarding, and as well as historic buildings and churches the restaurants both in Barr, near the temple, and around Largo Senado, are excellent.

is legal; the Chinese love to gamble and are travelling here in ever-increasing numbers. The arrival of Nevada-style casinos has transformed Macau into Asia's Las Vegas and the tiny enclave now earns more money from gaming than the Las Vegas Strip itself.

Sights in Macau

If you arrive from Hong Kong, The Sands casino in the outer harbour is one of the first sights you'll see in the 'new Macau'. Just in front of it is the **Fisherman's Wharf** theme park (www.fishermanswharf.com.mo; 24 hours; free; rides: 10am–9pm; charge) where replicas of European buildings, a Tang dynasty palace and an 'active' volcano house funfair rides, amusements, shops and restaurants. The grandstand, opposite the ferry terminal on **Avenida da Amizade**, marks the finishing line for the Macau Grand Prix, an international racing event held here every November.

The 'Historic Centre of Macau' was added to the Unesco World Heritage list in 2005, acknowledging its importance as the place where Eastern and Western culture first met, as well as its unique architectural heritage. Start your exploration at **Largo do Senado** (Senate Square). For an authentic feel of old Portugal, slip into the cool entrance hall of the impressive **Leal Senado** (Loyal Senate) building, a fine example of colonial architecture. Built in 1784, the inside walls are covered in flowered blue tiles *(azulejos)* and coats of arms. An inscription over the archway reads, '*Cidade do nome de Deus, não ha outra mais leal*' (City of the name of God, none is more loyal) – praise for Macau's loyalty during the Spanish occupation of Portugal in the 17th century, when the enclave refused to fly the aggressor's flag.

Macau's most memorable monument is the Baroque façade of the **Ruins of St Paul's** (São Paulo), the only remaining part of a beautiful 17th-century Jesuit church. On top of a hill in the centre of the city, it's approached by a grand staircase. The rest of the building, an adjoining college and nearby Monte Fortress were destroyed in a fire in 1835. The rich sculptural effects on the facade mix Eastern and Western symbols: saints, Chinese dragons and a Portuguese caravel.

The **Museum of Macau** (www.macaumuseum.gov.mo; Tue–Sun 10am–6pm; charge) is in the lower levels of the **Monte Fortress** (daily 7am–7pm), which was built by the Jesuits in the 17th century as a defence against the Dutch. Entrance is by an escalator, near St Paul's. The museum gives an overview of Macau's history and traditions.

In Largo do Senado

Luís Vaz de Camões (1524–80), the Portuguese national poet whose work immortalised the country's golden age of discoveries, may have stayed in Macau. Local legend claims that he wrote part of his great saga, *Os Lusíadas*, in what is now called the **Camões Grotto**, situated in the spacious tropical Camões Garden. Next to the garden, behind a gate (opened to anyone who knocks), is the **Old Protestant Cemetery**. Those whose fate it was to die on some far-flung field could not have wished for a more peaceful, lovely graveyard. The whitewashed chapel was the first Protestant church in China.

Lou Lim Ieoc Garden

For a taste of Old China, visit the classic **Lou Lim Ieoc Garden**. Bridges, pagodas, fish ponds and stands of bamboo create the mood of a timeless Chinese painting. Nearby is the **Memorial House of Dr Sun Yat-sen** (Wed–Mon 10am–5pm), founder of the Chinese Republic. Photos and documents tell the story of the physician-statesman, who lived for a time in Macau, but not in this building.

Kun Iam Tong (daily 7am–5.30pm), off Avenida do Coronel Mesquita, is a 17th-century Buddhist temple of considerable splendour and charm. Surrounded by statues, carvings and incense burners, the faithful make their devotions and check their fortunes, and traditional funerary displays give a cheerful send-off to the recently departed. An unexpected piece of historical memorabilia turns up in the monastery garden, where guides point out a small stone table used for a treaty-signing ceremony in 1844. The signatories – the Chinese viceroy from Canton and the minister plenipotentiary of the United States of America – put their names to a historic document, the first-ever treaty between the two countries.

On NAPE, a swathe of reclaimed land southwest of the ferry terminal, is the **Macau Cultural Centre**, with two auditoria and galleries, a core venue for the annual Macau Arts Festival in May. The adjacent **Museum of Art** (www. mam.gov.mo; Tue–Sun 10am–6.30pm; charge) houses more than 3,000 works, including permanent collections of paintings depicting the early days of East–West trade and historical images of Macau. Nearby, dominating the skyline on a small man-made causeway, stands a 20m (66ft) bronze **statue of Kun Iam**, by Portuguese artist Christina Reira. Underneath, in the dome-shaped lotus, is a small meditation centre and library.

Further along the shoreline, past MGM Macau, the One Central retail and office complex and the Nam Van Lakes, the **Macau Tower** stretches 338m (1,109ft) above the city. For a charge you can take a lift to the observation tower for panoramic views, and if you are brave you can walk around outside, climb the mast or try bungee jumping. There's a revolving restaurant on top of the tower, and in the adjoining convention cen-tre you will find a shopping plaza, more restaurants and a cinema.

Macau's oldest museum, the **Maritime Museum** (www.museumaritimo.gov. mo; Wed–Mon 10am–6pm; charge) traces the history of Macau's connection to the sea. Exhibits cover fishing,

Macau's Maritime Museum exhibits

seaborne trade and sea transport, and there is an aquarium. The museum also offers boat tours aboard a fishing junk.

The museum is almost on the spot where the Portuguese first landed. When they came ashore they found the **A-Ma Temple** (properly called Ma Kok Temple; daily dawn–dusk), dedicated to the favourite goddess of fishermen, who is also known as Tin Hau. The area was called A-Ma Gau (Bay of A-Ma), which is the source of Macau's name. The ornate, picturesque temple dates from the Ming Dynasty (1368–1644) and is the oldest building in Macau.

The strategically located **Barra Fortress** once defended the southern tip of the peninsula. Although not completed until 1627, it was instrumental in defending Macau's inner harbour against the 1622 attack by the Dutch. Used only once, the fort's cannons were exchanged for rice to feed World War II refugees. Part of the fortress is now a hotel, the Pousada de Sao Tiago, which contains the original **chapel of Sao Tiago** (St James), a saint much revered in the area.

The northernmost point in Macau is the frontier between two contrasting worlds. The **Barrier Gate** (Portas do Cerco), built more than a century ago, marks the boundary between the MSAR and the People's Republic of China.

Incense coils in A-Ma Temple

Casinos

Macau is famous for gambling and the new wave of Las Vegas-style casinos has added some pizzazz to its main revenue earner. The first of these newcomers was **Sands Macau** (www.

Macau's flashy Grand Lisboa casino

sandsmacao.com), with 277 gaming tables and 405 slot machines. Others, like the **Venetian**, **Galaxy Casino** and the **Greek Mythology** casino, complete with Roman centurions, offer plenty of spectacle. Kitsch old favourite **Lisboa** (www.hotellisboa.com) remains popular, but is dwarfed by the enormous **Wynn Macau**, **MGM Macau** and **Grand Lisboa**.

In packed halls, thousands of visitors, mainly Chinese, play familiar international games – blackjack, craps, roulette, baccarat – or hit the miles of slot machines. The 24-hour casinos have no admission charge and allow fairly casual dress, though men are required to wear long trousers. The gaming is the most important aspect of a visit.

If you want a change of scene there are always more gambling opportunities available. You can try greyhound-racing at the Canidrome (one of the largest in the world) or horse-racing on Taipa.

Balmy night dining on Coloane

Taipa and Coloane

Bridges link Macau to Taipa, which has its own ferry terminal as well as the Macau International Airport.

The quaint **Taipa Village**, with its narrow lanes and colonial buildings painted yellow, blue and green, has been almost completely swallowed up by the development of nearby housing estates. Be sure to pay a visit to the mint-green **Taipa Houses Museum** (www.housesmuseum.iacm.gov.mo; Tue–Sun 10am–6pm; charge), where five beautifully restored buildings house art galleries and museums. The island is also home to the University of East Asia.

The island of **Coloane** is now firmly connected to Taipa by Cotai, 80 hectares (200 acres) of reclaimed land dominated by Las Vegas Sands' 40-storey **Venetian Macao Resort Hotel**. It has 3,000 rooms, 55,000 sq m (600,000 sq ft) of casino space, a 15,000-seat sports arena, a permanent 1,500-seat theatre for Cirque de Soleil and an indoor life-size reproduction of St

Mark's Square. Next door is the sumptuous Four Seasons Macau. Across from Sands' Cotai Strip, Melco Crown Entertainment's **City of Dreams** (www.cityofdreamsmacau. com) is competing for punters with huge casinos and amazing immersive free shows at its giant theatre The Bubble. With a 1,000 sq m (10,764 sq ft) indoor playground, City of Dreams is also home to the Hard Rock Hotel Macau, Grand Hyatt Macau and the Crown Towers Macau. A spectacular 40-storey tower hotel designed by Zaha Hadid is due to open as part of the City of Dreams in 2017.

Once past the Cotai strip, Coloane is relatively undeveloped and its main attractions include a country park and beaches. Cheoc Van Beach and Hac Sa Beach (Black Sands) are both popular resort areas, with lifeguards on duty in summer, wind-surfing boards for hire, plus restaurants, swimming pools and changing facilities.

The 170m (560ft) peak of Coloane island is marked by a 20m (65ft) statue of the goddess A-Ma, which can be seen from the sea, and the **A-Ma Cultural Village** (daily 8am–6pm), a newly built Qing-dynasty-style complex with temples, bell tower, drum tower, Tian Hou Palace and museum.

The village of Coloane is peaceful and pretty. On the central square is the tiny chapel of **St Francis Xavier**, dedicated to the 16th-century saint. Eat at one of the cafés serving local food and walk down the waterfront along Avenida da Republica to the Kun Lam Temple, built in 1677 and dedicated to the gods of heaven, war, wealth and medicine.

St Francis Xavier chapel

WHAT TO DO

SHOPPING

Hong Kong loves shopping, so if you do too, you're going to love Hong Kong. And even if you aren't in thrall to the lure of the shopping gods, you will still enjoy the city's colourful markets and appreciate the efficiency of its air-conditioned malls (especially on a hot day, or the contrast and convenience of luxury brands' gigantic flagship stores a stone's throw from market stalls and alleyways selling cut-price seconds and knick-knacks. Perpetual browsers will find plenty of fascinating side streets to explore, too many to mention here, and determined bargain hunters will always be rewarded.

Since Hong Kong is a duty-free port with no sales tax, some goods are cheaper here than in their country of manufacture. On photographic equipment, electronic goods and watches, you avoid the luxury tax payable in your home country. Speciality goods and souvenirs, often handmade, come from Hong Kong and elsewhere in China. Garments custom-made by skillful Hong Kong tailors are still much in demand and cost less than elsewhere for comparable items. There are some exceptions to Hong Kong's duty-free regime, however – you will pay tax on tobacco and all alcohol except wine.

Stores do not open until 10am or later, but conversely stay open until 10pm or later. Most shops are open seven days a week. Stores in Central are an exception; they generally close at 7pm and on Sunday. The only holiday on which all commerce comes to a halt is the Chinese New Year in January or February.

Shopping in New Kowloon's markets

Looking for a good buy

Most stores have fixed prices, but it never hurts to ask for a discount or the 'best price', especially if you buy several items in a smaller shop or stall. Compare prices before you buy. Always ask to see the manufacturer's guarantee when purchasing cameras, watches, audio-visual and electronic equipment and check the box as it is packed. Note that when haggling, the merchant assumes you are prepared to pay cash. If, after making a deal, you try to pay with a credit card, they may then boost the price.

Shipping. Many stores will pack and ship purchases. Ask if automatic free insurance is provided. If the goods are very valuable or fragile, it is a good idea to buy an all-risk insurance for the shipment.

Where to shop

Major shopping areas are Tsim Sha Tsui in Kowloon, especially around Canton and Nathan roads; Central and Causeway Bay on Hong Kong Island; Wan Chai and Mong Kok markets for bargains rather than quality; and the Hollywood Road area for antiques.

Department stores. Look for Hong Kong's own Lane Crawford, a very upmarket store with branches at Pacific Place, IFC Mall and Harbour City; mid-range Wing On, one of the oldest in Hong Kong; the UK's Harvey Nichols in The Landmark and Marks & Spencer branches, and the Japanese stores, Sogo and Seibu.

Malls. Hong Kong is full of giant malls dedicated to shopping, eating and entertainment. Harbour City, just west of the Star Ferry Terminal in Tsim Sha Tsui, is one of the largest; Elements, above Kowloon MTR, is vast but quieter than most; IFC Mall and The Landmark in Central have major designer brands; Pacific Place in Admiralty has a mix of luxury and mid-range brands; and Times Square in Causeway Bay has 16 floors of spending opportunities.

Factory outlets. Hong Kong's garment factories have moved elsewhere, but there are still plenty of small outlets dotted about the city selling excess stock, samples and factory overruns. Try Johnston Road in Wan Chai, Fa Yuen Street in Mong Kok and Stanley Market. Pedder Building at 12 Pedder Street, Central has designer outlets. Also in Central, Li Yuen Street East and Li Yuen Street West, better known as 'The Lanes', have some outlet shops and all kinds of stalls selling chinoiserie, clothes, shoes, watches, bags and luggage.

Shopping tips

Be aware that name brands, including electronics, are sometimes fakes, glass may be sold as jade, and that antique you bought may have been made last night. Always ask for a receipt that records information about the item, and if you buy an antique, be sure to get a certificate of authentication. Needless to say, avoid peddlers who approach you in the street.

It is advisable to shop at outlets that are members of the Hong Kong Tourism Board's (HKTB) Quality Tourism Services Scheme, identified by a black Chinese character encircled by a golden letter Q with a small red junk in the bottom left corner. Membership imposes an obligation to maintain standards of both quality and service. For a list of qts-accredited outlets, pick up a copy of the HKTB's *A Guide to Quality Shops*. Look out for regular vip promotions and discounts that are only available to tourists.

Markets. Markets are the places to use your bargaining skills. Treat all claims of authenticity with a healthy pinch of salt, enjoy the banter and be prepared to walk away. Hong Kong's most famous and colourful market, selling every conceivable kind of goods, is the **Temple Street Night Market** near the Jordan MTR stop. By day the Ladies Market on Tung Choi Street, and nearby Fa Yuen Street in Mong Kok are the places to go for clothes and accessories. **Stanley Market** is located on Hong Kong's southern coast, and is good for men's, women's and children's clothes, shoes and gifts.

What to buy

Antiques. Hollywood Road, which runs from Central to Sheung Wan, is the most famous place for antiques in Hong Kong. Look for fine Chinese bronzes, embroidery, lacquerware and porcelain, tomb figures and wood carvings. The experts point out that it is not age alone that determines a Chinese antique's value – the dynasties of the past had their creative ups and downs. For genuine antiques, try Honeychurch Antiques at 29 Hollywood Road for furniture and silver or Tai Sing Company at 12 Wyndham Street for porcelain and pottery. For fun, you can visit the Low Price Shop at No. 47 or the Cat Street flea market. Horizon Plaza, 2 Lee Wing Street, Ap Lei Chau, Aberdeen is a vast industrial building with 27 floors of stores selling a mixture of Asian antiques, as well as modern and reproduction furniture.

Sales sales sales

Hong Kong has fantastic sales from just before Christmas until just after Chinese New Year and from mid-June through July.

Brocades and silks. Fabrics from China are a bargain and well worth taking home. Chinese-product department stores stock silk fabrics, silk scarves, finely embroidered blouses, and traditional padded jackets. Chinese Arts and Crafts is at Pacific Place in Central, and in Star House in Tsim Sha Tsui. For fabrics, you could try Western Market, Morrison Street, in Sheung Wan.

Cameras. Hong Kong is the place to buy some of the world's most advanced photographic equipment, and there are some real bargains around. However, be sure you compare prices and models before buying. Two reliable places to start looking in Central are Photo Scientific, 6 Stanley Street, and Hing Lee Camera Company, 25 Lyndhurst Terrace.

Chinese memorabilia at the Cat Street flea market

Carpets and rugs. Hong Kong is a mecca for handmade rugs from all over Asia. Caravan at 65 Hollywood Road, Horizon Plaza and The Silk Road at Ocean Centre, Harbour City in Tsim Sha Tsui are good places to start looking.

China (porcelain). Away from the antique stores of Hollywood Road and Horizon Plaza, China Arts & Crafts stores and the Wah Tung China Company at 7/F 57–9 Hollywood Road are good places to look for new items.

Electronics. The latest gadgets are sometimes available in Hong Kong before anywhere else. It's a great place to check out computers, cameras, video equipment, mobile phones, audio equipment and related accessories. Check prices online or at home before you browse and make sure you know what kind of guarantee you will get. Nathan Road has many electronics shops, but this is not where local people shop. Enter these shops if you know exactly what you want and what is the latest model. Fortress and Broadway are two reliable electronics chain stores that are safe to buy from, although a little bit more expensive than the smaller retailers. Also check out Star Computer City in Star House near the Star Ferry terminal in Kowloon. And no lover of technology should miss a visit to Wan Chai's computer malls at 138 and 298 Hennessy Road.

Furniture. The choice ranges from traditional hand-carved Chinese rosewood furniture to well-made reproductions of modern Western styles. Hollywood Road has more antique items, Horizon Plaza has furniture from all over Asia as well as modern designs, and Queen's Road East in Wan Chai has long been the place to go for furniture and soft furnishings.

Jade. 'Good for the health' is just one of the many qualities attributed to this beautiful stone, which ranges in colour from emerald green to white. Real jade is extremely expensive and some counterfeit jade looks exactly like the genuine article. Some people say you can test the authenticity by touch – real jade feels smooth and cool. Alternatively, you can shine a lamp on the stone – real jade shows no reflected light. Chinese Arts & Crafts stores give an indication of market prices, and the Jade Market in Yau Ma Tei is great fun.

Jewellery. Gold is top of the shopping list for many visitors from Asia and the packed stores are hard to miss. Other popular purchases include

Arts Festival

A highlight of the arts calendar is the annual Hong Kong Arts Festival (www.hk.arts festival.org), a three-week dose of international culture in February/March, with concerts, plays, Chinese opera, and other productions staged by leading talent from East and West. Tickets for the shows must be reserved well in advance.

Hong Kong is traditionally a good place to buy electronics

freshwater pearls and diamonds. At Rio Pearl, 3/F 39 Mody Road, you can buy gemstones loose or set, or have them made up to your own design. Gallery One, 31–3 Hollywood Road has an extensive range of semi-precious stones, beads, fixtures and fittings and will make jewellery to your design. Again, look out for the Q symbol that indicates the jewellery store has been accredited by the HKTB.

Kitchen equipment. Woks, bamboo steamers, biscuit moulds and other gadgets essential for Chinese cookery make good purchases. Shops on Bonham Strand, Sheung Wan and Shanghai Street, Yau Ma Tei, plus Yue Hwa Chinese Products Emporium, 301–9 Nathan Road, sell all sorts of intriguing kitchen equipment.

Leather goods. Bags and shoes are worshipped by many fashionistas in Hong Kong. Head to the malls for temples to Gucci, Louis Vuitton, Bottega Veneta and their rivals. Some people are also prepared to pay thousands for second-hand designer bags at Milan Station, at 26 Wellington Street, Central and at 10 other branches around the city.

Clothes. Hong Kong's shops carry almost every recognisable European and American label, from top-end designers to the moderately priced or on-trend brand. For clothes and accessories from young Hong Kong and Asian designers, visit the city's malls and markets, but you should also try small boutiques in and around SoHo. Shanghai Tang (12 Pedder Street, Central and 1881 Heritage TST) has classy Chinese inspired clothes and gifts.

Tea. If you want to learn something about tea, go to the Moon Garden Tea House at 5 Hoi Ping Road, Causeway Bay. The owners will brew up a pot so that you can taste before making a choice. There are tea classes at the Lock Cha Tea Shop in Hong Kong Park on weekdays (www.lockcha.com). For current schedule and fees call tel: 2805 1360.

ENTERTAINMENT

Hong Kong is a city that never sleeps and plenty of bars and eating places stay open well into the early hours. The Hong Kong Tourism Board offices and many hotels carry two free

Tailoring

Tailor-made clothes are not as popular in Hong Kong as they once were, but there are still many tailors' shops, experts when it comes to producing custom-made garments for men and women, and also adept at copying patterns. The result can be a quality suit at a fair price – but made-to-measure clothing is not cheap. Many tailors are located around Nathan Road and Mody Road in Tsim Sha Tsui. On Hong Kong Island, Tai Pan Row Tailors in IFC Mall and at 9 Queen's Road Central are a respected choice.

monthly magazines, *Citylife* and *Where*, which give night-life and restaurant listings as well as a run-down on what's showing at theatres and cinemas. Otherwise you can simply wander through the maze of neon signs and take your pick. For slightly more objective reviews of bars, restaurants and shows, study the City section of the *South China Morning Post*, the weekly *HK Magazine* or *BC Magazine* which comes out every two weeks. These last two are handed out free in many bars, restaurants and bookshops. There's always a varied programme of events, ranging from world-class concerts to local amateur dramatic productions.

Chinese opera

There are more than 30 cinemas in Hong Kong and the latest Western releases are shown in some of the larger ones. English-language films have Chinese subtitles. Mainland Chinese and foreign films usually have Cantonese and English subtitles. The **Hong Kong International Film Festival** (www.hkiff.org.hk) takes place in March/April. More than 200 films from all over the world are shown at this event.

The performing arts

Performance venues. The theatres in the **Hong Kong Cultural Centre** in Tsim Sha Tsui are the main venues for concerts and opera. Other performing arts centres are the **City Hall** (www.cityhall.gov.hk) cultural complex, with exhibition halls and theatres that present concerts, plays and films; the

The Hong Kong Dance Company in performance

Hong Kong Academy for Performing Arts (www.hkapa. edu) with two major theatres for dance, drama and concert performances; and the **Hong Kong Arts Centre** (www.hkac.org. hk) in Wan Chai. Other centres for concerts and entertainment are Sha Tin Town Hall, Kwai Tsing Theatre in Kwai Chung and the theatres in the Fringe Club for plays and cabaret. Larger arenas, including the Queen Elizabeth Stadium, the Hong Kong Coliseum, and the Ko Shan Theatre in Kowloon play host to various concerts, sporting events and variety shows.

Classical music. The Hong Kong Chinese Orchestra (www.hkco.org) performs new and traditional works featuring traditional and Chinese instruments. The Hong Kong Philharmonic (www.hkphil.org) performs Western classical works and new pieces by Chinese composers in its September-to-June season.

Chinese opera. Cantonese opera is alive and well in Hong Kong, and the two other forms, Beijing and Kunju, are sometimes presented as well. For most foreigner visitors, this unique art form is likely to be inscrutable at first exposure, but everyone can appreciate the spectacle and the elaborate, glittering costumes. Although the music may seem strange to the unaccustomed ear, its loud cymbals and drums certainly won't send you to sleep.

Dance. Hong Kong's three professional dance companies – the Hong Kong Ballet Company, the Hong Kong Dance Company and the newer City Contemporary Dance Company – perform regularly, often at the Hong Kong Academy for Performing Arts.

Theatre. The two leading local troupes, the Chung Ying Theatre Company and the Hong Kong Repertory Theatre, always perform in Cantonese, but there are also some English-language performances at the Fringe Club, in Central, and some amateur productions are staged at the Arts Centre.

Nightlife

Hong Kong by night can suit any taste – riotous, sedate, raw, or cultured. Sometimes there is a cover charge of HK$50–200 at clubs, which may or may not include a couple of drinks. Many of Hong Kong's five-star hotels have bars with live music and some of the best views in

Night cruises

Star Ferry (www.starferry.com.hk) offers a two-hour harbour cruise, departing TST pier at 7pm each evening, timed to take in the 8pm Symphony of Lights. Aqua Luna (Central Pier 9, TST Star Ferry Pier; www.aqualuna.com.hk), a traditional red-sailed junk, has harbour cruises every hour in the evenings and some weekday afternoons. Lamma Island's Rainbow Restaurant, Sok Kwu Wan (www.rainbowrest.com.hk), offers a free evening shuttle for patrons from Central Pier 9.

Sailing on the Aqua Luna

the city. The Lobster Bar at the Island Shangri-La is one of the classiest places for live music. The Sky Lounge, on the 18th floor of the Sheraton, and the glitzy Lobby Lounge at the InterContinental, with floor-to-ceiling harbour views, are great places to take in the Symphony of Lights (8pm), a sound and light display, starring the Hong Kong Island skyline.

The Fringe Club (www.hkfringe.com.hk), 21 Lower Albert Road, Central is Hong Kong's best alternative entertainment venue, with jazz, rock and other live music, in addition to an excellent gallery for visual arts and a relaxing rooftop bar. Pubs are numerous. In Tsim Sha Tsui, Ned Kelly's Last Stand on Ashley Road is an Aussie institution and Delaney's, at 71–7 Peking Road, is one of Hong Kong's enduring Irish pubs.

The clubs and bars of **Wan Chai**, long the centre of seedy nightlife, have become almost respectable. Dusk til Dawn,

76–84 Jaffe Road, is a Wan Chai mainstay for all-night partying. Mes Amis (www.mesamis.com.hk) at 81–5 Lockhart Road, has a lively dance floor at the weekend. A lot of the raunchy action has moved across the harbour to Tsim Sha Tsui East; this is also where you'll find pricey hostess clubs.

SoHo (South of Hollywood Road) is a hip area, which spreads around the Central Mid-Levels escalator, to Elgin, Peel and Staunton Streets and Hollywood Road. SoHo, The area has a great choice of restaurants and a lively bar scene. Staunton's (www.stauntonsgroup.com) at 10–12 Staunton Street, the rooftop bar at The Fringe Club and Hong Kong Brew House (www.elgrande.com.hk) at the top of Lan Kwai Fong are good places to take in the scene.

Causeway Bay is packed with restaurants and bars to visit after late-night shopping. ToTTs in the Excelsior Hotel is a more sophisticated restaurant with music and an outdoor terrace, while the small bars in the streets around Times Square attract a younger crowd.

SPORTS AND OUTDOOR ACTIVITIES

Beaches. In subtropical Hong Kong you can swim from April to early November, but water quality depends on tidal and climatic problems. Aside from concerns about pollution, rubbish in the water is all too common. There are more than 40 government-managed beaches with lifeguards, shark nets, changing rooms, showers, toilets and water testing (Apr–Oct). On Hong Kong Island, Repulse Bay is the most popular; others are Shek O on the east coast, and Stanley and Deep Water Bay on the south coast. They are very crowded, especially at summer weekends. On the outlying islands, Cheung Sha is on Lantau, Tung Wan is on Cheung Chau and Hung Shing Ye and Lo So Shing are on Lamma.

Golf. The Hong Kong Golf Club (tel: 2670 1211; www.hkgolfclub.org) has three 18-hole courses at Fanling in the New Territories. The Discovery Bay Golf Club on Lantau island (tel: 2987 7273; www.dbgc.hk) has three nine-hole courses. Both are open to the public on weekdays. Kau Sai Chau (tel: 2791 3388; www.kscgolf.org.hk) run by the Jockey Club is the only public golf course in Hong Kong and enjoys a spectacular island location in the New Territories (see page 59). Many Hong Kong residents and visitors cross the border to play at the less expensive world-class courses in Guangdong: the Guangzhou Luhu Golf and Country Club (www.luhugolf.com), or Mission Hills Resort (www.missionhillsgroup.com).

Hiking. In the New Territories the famous MacLehose Trail stretches 97km (60 miles) from Sai Kung Peninsula to Tuen Mun. The Lantau Trail is a 69km (43-mile) circular trail on

A night at Happy Valley is a classic experience

Lantau Island that begins and ends at Silvermine Bay. Both trails are divided into segments of varying difficulty. Trail maps are available at the Government Publications Centre, Low Block, Government Offices, 66 Queensway in Central. HKTB also has maps and sponsors the Guided Nature Walks, that include hikes in all regions of Hong Kong.

Waymarked trails

Taijiquan (t'ai chi). The HKTB offers free lessons in these exercises that improve concentration and balance. They start at 8am near the Cultural Centre at the Avenue of Stars in Tsim Sha Tsui. Contact the HKTB for further information.

Horseracing. The racing schedule is September to June, and the Jockey Club (www.hkjc.com) runs two courses, Happy Valley on Hong Kong Island (see page 39) and Sha Tin (see page 57). Dress like a racehorse owner and join the HKTB's 'Come Horseracing Tour', which includes entry to the Jockey Club visitors' box and members' enclosure, and a meal. For a more casual day or night at the races, the public stands have no dress code and the entrance cost is HK$10.

Cricket and rugby. International cricket sixes events are a regular part of the sporting calendar each autumn. The Hong Kong Rugby Sevens has become the world's premier sevens tournament. For one weekend in late March or early April the Hong Kong Stadium hosts international teams and fans who come for the party as much as the sport.

CHILDREN'S HONG KONG

Hong Kong has many attractions that appeal to children of all ages. Apart from the theme parks and beaches, there are many novelties. Cable-car rides are usually popular, a ride on the Peak Tram is sure to provide a thrill, and children will enjoy the various attractions in the Peak Tower, including Madame Tussauds (see page 29). Riding the Star Ferry or ferry trips to outlying islands are inexpensive fun, and the Dolphin Watch trip (see page 120) is certain to appeal.

Ocean Park (see page 41) is very popular with children of all ages and may warrant two visits. Hong Kong

Thrills at Ocean Park

Disneyland (see page 62), is easily reached aboard the special Disneyland Resort MTR train.

Indoor activities at the Science Museum in Tsim Sha Tsui East allow children to get their hands on more than half the 500 exhibits, while the nearby Space Museum has regular movie screenings on an OmnIMAX screen.

The carnival atmosphere of the Cheung Chau Bun Festival, with its high bamboo-and-paper towers covered in steamed buns, held in May, and the Dragonboat races in June will fascinate youngsters, as will the full-moon festival in September.

Calendar of Festivals

Precise dates cannot be given as Chinese festivals are fixed according to the lunar calendar.

January/February: *Lunar New Year.* A three-day holiday when Chinese families get together. Flower markets are particularly colourful and temples are packed with worshippers. People hand out *lai see* (lucky money packets) to children. There's a huge parade on the first day of the new year, and an elaborate fireworks display over the harbour on the second.

April: *Ching Ming Festival.* This Confucian festival, timed to the solar calendar, is one of two annual holidays to honour the dead. Ancestors' graves are swept and offerings of food, wine or flowers are made.

April/May: *Tin Hau Festival.* The Taoist Goddess of the Sea is honoured by fishing communities, especially at Joss House Bay, where decorated junks and sampans converge with offerings. Smaller celebrations, including lion-dancing, take place elsewhere.

May: *Birthday of the Lord Buddha.* In Buddhist temples the Buddha's image is bathed in scented water to symbolise the washing away of sins. Ngong Ping and Po Lin have special events. *Cheung Chau Bun* Festival is celebrated by the erection of bamboo towers piled with some 5,000 pink and white lotus-paste buns. It lasts for five or nine days and includes processions, lion and dragon dances and traditional temple rites.

May/June: *Dragon Boat Festival (Tuen Ng).* Oarsmen in long, thin dragon boats race to the beat of big bass drums and Chinese gongs. Annual International Dragon Boat races are held a few days after the festival.

August: *Seven Sisters' (Maidens') Festival.* Women wanting husbands leave offerings at Lovers' Rock. *Hungry Ghosts Festival (Yue Lan).* Paper offerings are burned and food left out to placate ghosts.

September: *Mid-Autumn Festival.* As the full moon rises, tots carrying paper lanterns congregate in open spaces or high places and eat moon cakes (ground sesame and lotus seeds or dates).

October: *Cheung Yeung Festival.* On the ninth day of the ninth moon, people visit ancestors' graves and try to reach a high place for luck.

EATING OUT

The Chinese care about food with a passion that perhaps only the French can rival. For the Chinese, eating is a pleasure imbued with philosophical profundities: even the dead are offered food and wine to make their journey more peaceful.

Restaurants are a place for family and social gatherings. Eating out is one of the main forms of socialising, and the Chinese usually eat in large groups. If Chinese hosts invite you to a restaurant, put yourself in their hands; they will try to order according to their impression of your tastes.

Chefs have a demanding clientele. All Chinese consider themselves gourmets and demand not only the best flavours but colour, texture and presentation to enhance the pleasure of the food. A real Chinese meal is orchestrated, and must contain a harmonious progression from sweet to sour, crunchy to tender. A Chinese banquet is a triumph of the well-rounded art of food.

You will find restaurants serving food from all over China, Asia and the world. The long-established Indian community means there are many excellent Indian restaurants; Thai and Vietnamese cuisine is well represented; and Hong Kong's love of Japanese and Korean culture means there are some great places for sushi and Korean barbecues. Among the most popular international cuisines are Italian, French, Middle Eastern, Mexican and American-style steakhouses and there are plenty of international and local fast-food and coffee shop chains. Swiss, Austrian, Burmese, Ukrainian and African restaurants are some of the more unusual finds here. Vegetarians do not have an easy time in Cantonese restaurants as most Chinese chefs

Rice to meet you

A common Cantonese greeting is 'Lay sik jaw fan may ah?' – ('Have you had your rice yet?')

use chicken or other meat stock routinely in otherwise vegetarian dishes, but there are a growing number of dedicated vegetarian restaurants.

Meal times

Most hotels serve a breakfast buffet of Chinese and Western food from about 7 to 10am. At lunchtime business people pack the restaurants from 1 to 2pm. Dinner is between 7.30 and 9.30pm, but restaurants are flexible; many are open from early in the morning until midnight without a break.

Digging in to noodles

A traditional Chinese breakfast consists of *congee*, a rice gruel or porridge to which almost anything may be added. At backstreet breakfast stalls you will also see the early risers digging into noodle soup with chunks of vegetable or pork.

Regional cuisines

Chinese food comes in half a dozen principal styles, all very different. In Hong Kong every major school of Chinese cooking is represented; restaurants have inherited recipes and brilliant cooks from all parts of China.

Cantonese

For visitors, this is probably the most familiar Chinese cuisine, as so many Cantonese emigrated, opened restaurants

A typical Cantonese vegetable side dish

and introduced new tastes to diners in the West. Cantonese food is either steamed or stir-fried, cooking methods that capture the flavour of the ingredients as well as the colour and vitamins. A vast range of ingredients is used, and the flavours are many and often delicately understated.

A Cantonese seafood dinner often includes fresh fish steamed with ginger, spring onions and soy sauce, with a touch of garlic. Prawns steamed with garlic, clams with black bean sauce and scallops cooked with garlic are all popular choices. A green vegetable such as *choi sum*, *bak choi* or broccoli with garlic or oyster sauce is a good accompaniment. Soup is usually served towards the end of the meal – sweetcorn and crabmeat soup is one of the most popular. Steamed white rice is normally served with a Cantonese meal.

Chiu Chow

This regional cuisine from the Swatow region of southeast China excels in novel seasonings and rich sauces. Chefs also pride themselves on their amazing vegetable carvings that are part of every Chiu Chow banquet. Before and after dinner you will be presented with tiny cups of a strong and bitter tea, known as Iron Buddha.

Two very expensive Chiu Chow delicacies are shark's fin and birds' nest (but note that sharks have become endangered because of over-fishing). A typical dish is minced pigeon:

the pigeon meat is minced and fried with herbs, and eaten wrapped in lettuce leaves. In Chiu Chow restaurants congee is often served instead of rice.

Beijing (Peking)

The Chinese emperors made Beijing the gourmet centre of the country, and Hong Kong's Peking restaurants still present truly imperial banquets (ordered in advance) with everything from nuts to soup, in that order. Northern food tends to be richer than Cantonese food. Don't miss one of the world's most delicious eating experiences, Peking duck. The duck is honey-coated before roasting and is cut at the table. The celebrants put chunks of the crisp skin along with spring onions and a sweet sauce onto delicate pancakes, which are then rolled up and devoured. The meat is then taken away

Chinese dining offers a wide variety of experiences, from humble street food to gourmet cuisine with a view

to be stir fried with other ingredients and served as a separate dish.

Wheat, not rice, is the staple in northern China. Peking restaurants serve noodles and various kinds of bread, and also specialise in delicious dumplings, stuffed with meat or vegetables.

Roasted duck is a common sight at market stalls

Shanghai

Shanghai food is an amalgam of a number of Chinese cuisines from surrounding cities. It tends to be more diverse and complicated as well as more thoroughly cooked than Cantonese. Chili peppers, garlic and ginger are used in moderation. Freshwater hairy crab, imported from Shanghai in autumn, is steamed and eaten with the hands. Cold dishes are more popular, too and one essential dish is *xiao long bao*, a Chinese-style bun filled with a mixture of minced pork, ginger, spring onion and a spoonful of soup. Shanghai diners usually prefer noodles to rice.

Beggar's chicken

Some Beijing and Shanghai restaurants also serve a dish known as 'beggar's chicken' thought to originate in Hangzhou. According to legend, the inventor was a tramp who stole a chicken but had no way to cook it. After tossing in some salt and onion, he covered the entire bird in a shell of mud, then roasted it on a fire. When the mud was baked dry he smashed the coating, the feathers came off with the clay and all the juicy tenderness of the bird remained. The recipe has become more sophisticated as mushrooms, pickled cabbage, shredded pork, bamboo shoots and wine are added to the stuffing. Now the chicken is served in clay at the table, and smashed on the spot.

Sichuan

This food from southwestern China is chili-laden and spicy. It produces such sharp, hot flavours that it first takes your breath away, then awakens your palate. Once the fiery shock of the garlic-enhanced chili peppers has subsided, you can distinguish the many other elements in unlikely coexistence – bitter, sweet, fruity, tart and sour.

Smoked duck, Sichuan style, is marinated in rice wine, with ginger and an array of spices, then steamed before being smoked over a specially composed wood fire. Equally delicious is deep-fried beef with vegetables, a dish in which the meat and most of the other ingredients –carrots, celery, peppers, garlic – are shredded and slowly fried over a low flame.

Chopsticks

You'll lose face – and fun – if you don't learn to use chopsticks to eat your food in Hong Kong. There's no reason to feel self-conscious – the Chinese are tolerant when it comes to table manners.

Begin by settling the bottom stick firmly at the conjunction of the thumb and forefinger, balancing it against the first joint of the ring finger. The second stick pivots around the fulcrum made by the tip of the thumb and the inside of the forefinger.

Remember not to lay your chopsticks across each other, and never place them across the rice bowl, but rest them on the holder provided or against a plate.

Knives and forks are supplied in most restaurants. If it's any consolation, many Chinese don't feel quite at home with them either.

Traditional dim sum service

Hakka

The name Hakka means 'guest people', referring to their migration to this region from northern China many centuries ago. Hakka cuisine involves the use of simple ingredients, especially versatile bean curd. Look for an ingenious dish called salted chicken; a coating of salt contains and increases the flavours while the bird is being baked.

Dim sum

Late breakfast or lunch can consist of tea and dim sum, the small snacks that add up to a delicious and filling meal. Servers wander from table to table chanting the Cantonese names of the foods contained in bamboo steamers on their trays or carts. Choose whatever looks interesting – from spring rolls to spare ribs and dozens of different varieties of dumplings, including *siu mui* (pork and shrimp dumplings), *har gau* (delicate steamed shrimp dumplings), and *cha siu bau* (little barbecued pork buns).

Drinks

Since the beginning of the 21st century the Chinese have taken to drinking wine with enthusiasm. Red wines are the most popular, with French Bordeaux possessing the most cachet, but wine from elsewhere in Europe, Australia, New Zealand and the Americas is widely available. In an attempt to encourage more lucrative wine auctions to be held in the city, tax on wine was abolished in 2008, so prices are reasonable.

The Chinese have been making wine for 4,000 years and some mainland producers have entered into partnerships with foreign companies. The popular brand Dynasty is working with Remy Cointreau and is showing promise.

Other than wine made with grapes, rice wine and wheat-based wines are notorious for their alcoholic power. Mao Tai is a breathtaking case in point.

Tsingtao beer from China has a hearty European taste. You'll also find a large selection of European and American brands, some of them brewed locally under licence. The locally brewed San Miguel is cheap and refreshing.

The Chinese have been drinking tea for many centuries as a thirst-quencher, general reviver, and ceremonial beverage. Tea in China is drunk without sugar or milk, although 'English-style' tea is available. It's worth making the effort to learn to appreciate the many varieties of tea and their histories. For a caffeine-free alternative, ask for hot chrysanthemum tea, brewed from the dried petals of the flower.

Rounding off the beverage list are familiar soft drinks and a range of tasty tropical fruit juices. Coffee can be enjoyed throughout the city at chains like Starbucks, Pacific Coffee and Delifrance.

Thousand-year eggs

The famous 'thousand-year eggs' are duck eggs buried in lime for 60 days, with a resulting cheese-like taste.

TO HELP YOU ORDER...

Waiter!/Waitress! **Mgoi!**

Have you a table? **Yau mo toi ah?**

Do you have a set menu? **Yau mo to chaan a?**

I'd like a/an/some... **Ngor seung yiu...**

The bill, please. **Mai dan, m goi.**

beer **bei jau**	ice **bing**
beef **ngau yuk**	lamb **yurng yuk**
cake **daan go**	menu **chan pye**
chicken **gai**	pork **ju-ee yuk**
chopsticks **fai ji**	rice **faan**
cup **bui**	steak **ngau pa**
dessert **tim bun**	soup **tong**
fish **yue**	tea **cha**
fruit **sang gwo**	water **sui**
glass **bor lay bui**	wine **jau**

...AND READ THE MENU

蟹肉豆腐羹	bean curd and crabmeat soup
麻婆豆腐	bean curd with pork in pepper sauce
合桃鷄丁	diced chicken with walnuts
腰果肉丁	diced pork with cashew nuts
干燒冬筍	fried bamboo shoots and cabbage
炒鱔糊	fried eel with soya sauce
清炒蝦仁	fried shrimps
青椒肉絲	fried sliced pork with green pepper
菜扒鮮菇	mushrooms with vegetables
辣子鷄丁	shredded chicken with green pepper
豉椒牛肉	sliced beef with green pepper and bean sauce
三絲湯	sliced chicken, abalone and prawn soup
紅燒魚片	sliced fish with brown sauce
糟溜黃魚	stewed yellow fish
咕嚕肉	sweet and sour pork
鷄油津白	Tientsin cabbage and asparagus

PLACES TO EAT

We have used the following symbols to give an idea of the price for a three-course meal (or Asian equivalent) per person, not including alcoholic drinks:

$$$$ over HK$600   **$$** HK$150–300

$$$ HK$300–600   **$** below HK$150

KOWLOON

Fat Angelo's $–$$ *Shop B, Basement, The Pinnacle, 8 Minden Avenue, Tsim Sha Tsui, tel: 2730 4788, www.fatangelos.com, daily noon–midnight.* A friendly, uncomplicated American-Italian restaurant dishing up huge portions that can feed up to eight people. Children get an activity menu, but it also serves as a romantic setting with its checked tablecloths and wine served in tumblers. Other branches at 1 Belcher's Street in Kennedy Town and Panda Hotel at Panda Place in Tsuen WAn.

Felix $$$$ *The Peninsula, Salisbury Road, tel: 2696 6778, www. peninsula.com, daily from 6pm, with last food orders at 10.30pm.* This restaurant is not to be missed: the marvellous view and the striking Philippe Starck design are nearly as important as the food. The Pacific Rim fusion cuisine is delectable.

Spice Restaurant and Bar $$ *2/Floor, 1 Knutsford Terrace, Tsim Sha Tsui, tel: 2191 9880; www.spice-restaurant.hk, daily noon–3pm, 6pm–midnight.* This contemporary restaurant offers a perfect fusion of Indian, Thai and Malaysian cuisine. A vibrant ambience and lively atmosphere makes it one of the best and most popular venues on Knutsford Terrace.

Dragon Seal $$$ *International Commerce Centre, 1 Austin Road West, West Kowloon, tel: 2568 9886, www.shkp-icc.com, daily 11.30am–11.30pm.* Located on the 101st floor of ICC, this is fabulous for views of the harbour and the city. The classic dim sum dishes with modern twist are tasteful and well prepared.

Jade Garden Restaurant $$ *4/F Star House, Tsim Sha Tsui, tel: 2730 6888, www.maximeschinese.com.hk, Mon–Sat11am–4pm, 6–11pm, Sunday 10am–4pm, 6–11.30pm.* Classic dishes, dim sum and seasonal specialities available. Ask for the dishes of the day.

Jimmy's Kitchen $$ *Kowloon Centre, 29 Ashley Road, Tsim Sha Tsui, tel: 2376 0327, www.jimmys.com, daily noon–2.30pm, 6–11pm.* One of Hong Kong's oldest restaurants, it specialises in British food, but has curries and other Asian dishes. There's also a branch at 1–3 Wyndham Street in Central.

Chi Lin Vegetarian $$ *Nan Lian Garden, 60 Fung Tak Road, Diamond, tel: 3658 9388, daily 11.30am–9pm.* It is hard to find strictly vegetarian Chinese food as most chefs add meat broth to vegetarian dishes. This restaurant is one of a handful that specialises in true vegetarian meals. It's beautifully situated in a traditional Buddhist Garden.

Nha Trang $ *Shop G51 Ground Floor, Ocean Terminal, Harbour City, Tsim Sha Tsui, tel: 2199 7779, www.nhatrang.com.hk, daily noon–4.45pm, 6.15–11pm.* Low prices and dishes bursting with flavourful spices and herbs make this an enjoyable place to eat Vietnamese food. Try their addictive *pho* with noodles and beef or chicken, fresh rice paper rolls with grilled prawns and crispy skinned suckling pig. Service is patchy, but people keep going back. Branches in Central and Wan Chai are equally good, but this one has the harbour view.

Sorabol Korean Restaurant $$ *4/F Miramar Shopping Centre, 1 Kimberley Road, Tsim Sha Tsui, tel: 2375-2882, www.sorabol.com.hk, daily 11.30am–3pm and 6–10pm.* One of Hong Kong's best Korean restaurants, where authentic dishes draw in the local Korean community. Have barbecue at your table or order à la carte. If there's a queue, make a booking and head to Knutsford Terrace for a drink while you wait.

Spring Deer $$ *1/F 42 Mody Road, Tsim Sha Tsui, tel: 2366 4012, daily 8–11pm, 2–?am.* A Hong Kong institution, Spring Deer has been in the same location for over three decades, While the decor is tired, the friendly staff are not, serving up mainly northern-Chinese food. The Peking duck with pancakes and all the trimmings is unmissable.

Tai Woo Restaurant $ *14–16 Hillwood Road, Tsim Sha Tsui, tel: 2368 5420, www.taiwoorestaurant.com, daily until 3am.* Popular favourites at this restaurant include seafood dishes such as steamed garoupa or sautéed scallops. The set meals are a good way of sampling a range of Cantonese dishes.

Yan Toh Heen $$$$ *InterContinental Hotel, 18 Salisbury Road, Tsim Sha Tsui, tel: 2313 2323, Mon–Sat noon–2.30pm and 6–11pm, Sun until 3pm.* This elegant restaurant with opulent decor and great views over the harbour serves exquisite and innovative Cantonese and Chinese food.

CENTRAL

Beirut $$–$$$ *G/F–1/F, 27–39 D'Aguilar Street, Lan Kwai Fong, Central, tel: 2804 6611, www.beirutbar.com, daily 11am–2pm, 6pm until late.* This restaurant offers an extensive menu of Lebanese specialities, including *shawarma* and *lahme bil agine* (a kind of Lebanese pizza). The home-made hummus is the best in Hong Kong. Ideal for lunch.

The Grand Stage $$ *2/F Western Market, 323 Des Voeux Road, Sheung Wan, tel: 2815 2311, daily 11.30am–3pm, 7pm–midnight.* This good Cantonese restaurant is located in an attractive Western Market building that dates back to 1906. Great for dim sum or lunch after exploring historic Sheung Wan. After lunch some tables are pushed back and ballroom dancers take to the floor.

Habibi Café $–$$ *112–114 Wellington Street, Central, tel: 2544 3886, www.habibi.com.hk, daily 11am–midnight.* This tiny café offers authentic Egyptian food with a selection of hot and cold meze, tasty lamb shashlik, moussaka and plenty of vegetarian choices. Its sister restaurant in Lan Kwai Fong (Habibi, 1/F, Grand Progress Building) offers equally excellent food in a more spacious setting, plus belly dancing.

IR1968 $$ *5/F The L. Place, 139 Queens Road Central, tel: 2577 9981, www.ir1968.com.* This Indonesian restaurant first opened in 1968 – hence the name – but has had a facelift and is now a pretty funky joint. It serves authentic Indonesian food, presented in a modern way, including *nasi goring* and chicken curry.

Isola Bar and Grill $$$$, *Level Two, IFC Mall, Finance Street, Central, tel: 2383 8765, www.isolabarandgrillcom, Mon–Thur 11.30am–11pm, Fri–Sat noon–11.30pm, Sun noon–10.30pm.* Modern Italian cuisine with a stunning harbour view.

Jashan $$ *1/F 23 Hollywood Road, Central, tel: 3105 5300, www.jashan.com.hk, Sun–Thur noon–midnight, Fri–Sat noon–2am.* Extensive menu with dishes from north and south India. The richly decorated restaurant serves a good-value lunch.

Kiku Japanese Restaurant $$$ *1st Basement, Gloucester Tower, The Landmark, Des Voeux Road Central, tel: 2521 3344, www.landmark.hk, Mon–Sat 11.30am–3pm, 6–10.30pm, Sun noon–3pm, 6–10.30pm.* A traditional pine-panelled restaurant serving *teppanyaki* and sushi delicacies. The à la carte menu features Kyoto-style cuisine; grilled codfish and eel are recommended.

Luk Yu Tea House $$$ *24 Stanley Street, tel: 2523 5464, daily 7am–9pm (dim sum until 6pm).* This place has been around for 60 years, and is a living piece of colonial history with its carved wooden doors and panelling. It is a popular venue for excellent dim sum.

Masala $ *10 Mercer Street, Sheung Wan, tel: 2581 9777.* Close to Sheung Wan MTR, between Bonham Strand and Jervois Street, this tiny restaurant is worth seeking out for its extensive choice of Indian dishes at very reasonable prices. Modern decor and friendly, helpful service add to the experience. Favourites include *bhindi masala*, fish madras, *tarka dhal* and tandoori chicken; the set menus offer remarkable value; enjoy with reasonably priced Australian wine, a cold Kingfisher beer or *lassi*.

THE PEAK

Café Deco $$–$$$ *1/F and 2/F Peak Galleria, 118 Peak Road, tel: 2849 5111, www.cafedecogroup.com, Sun–Thur 11am–11pm, Fri–Sat 11am–11.30pm.* Set at the top of Hong Kong Island for more than a decade, Café Deco's open kitchen prepares international cuisine to please all tastes from steaks and seafood to made-to-share platters of Italian, Indian, Thai and Japanese favourites. Book ahead and be sure to request tables with the best views of Hong Kong.

Pearl on the Peak $$$$ *Level 1, The Peak Tower, 128 Peak Road, tel: 2849 5123, www.maxconcepts.com.hk, daily noon–2.30pm, 6–11 pm.* Modern Australian/international food, based on Melbourne's award-winning Pearl restaurant. The top location, plus floor-to-ceiling glass walls, means you get spectacular views. The food is sensational, leaning towards southeast Asian and Mediterranean flavours.

WAN CHAI

American Restaurant $ *Golden Star Building G/F-2/F, 20 Lockhart Road, tel: 2527 7277, daily 11am–11pm.* Popular restaurant for four decades, specialising in northern Chinese dishes, and a favourite venue for visitors and nostalgic locals. Rumour has it the name changed to American, to attract US servicemen on R&R in Hong Kong in the 1960s. Plenty of noodles, Kung Pao prawns and the Peking duck.

Cinta J $$ *69 Jaffe Road, tel: 2529 6622, daily 11am–5am.* A friendly restaurant serving Indonesian favourites such as satay, prawn chili, fried squid and beef Rendang. Filipino dishes include crispy pata (pork leg) and mixed adobo. There are also Malaysian favourites. Live music nightly.

Fook Lam Moon $$$–$$$$ *35–45 Johnston Road, tel: 2866 0663, www.fooklammoon-grp.com, daily 11.30am–3pm, 6–10pm.* One of the top Cantonese restaurants in the city. Seafood is the speciality. Also at 53–9 Kimberley Road in Tsim Sha Tsui.

The Pawn $–$$$ *2 & 3/F 62 Johnston Road, Wan Chai, tel: 2866 3444, www.thepawn.com.hk, Living Room 11am–midnight; Dining Room noon–3pm, 6pm–midnight.* Three traditional shop houses were saved from the wreckers' ball and converted into this beautiful venue with original features from local pawnshops. Food in the second-floor Dining Room is 'modern British'. Those in the know order bar snacks and park themselves in huge wicker chairs on the first floor Living Room's balcony to watch the Wan Chai world go by.

Tamarind $$–$$$ *2/F, Sun Hung Kai Centre, 30 Harbour Road, tel: 2827 7777, www.chiram.com.hk, daily 11am–11pm.* This spacious restaurant has combined two venues and cuisines. Choose from outstanding Indian, Thai and Vietnamese cuisine and enjoy spectacular panoramic harbour views from an outdoor terrace.

CAUSEWAY BAY

Cammino Restaurant $$ *1/F, The Excelsior, 281 Gloucester Road, Causeway Bay, tel: 2837 6780, www.mandarinoriental.com, Mon–Sat noon–2.15pm, 6–10.15pm, Sun brunch 11.30am–3pm.* Popular Italian restaurant offering classic and modern dishes. Try the Spinosini pasta with lamb ragout and cherry tomatoes.

Kung Tak Lam Shanghai Vegetarian Cuisine $ *10/F World Trade Centre, Causeway Bay, tel: 2881 9966, daily 11am–11pm.* This long-standing vegetarian restaurant has moved from a back street to a lively shopping mall near Causeway Bay MTR, and now has views of the harbour. Extensive choice of dishes including Buddhist-style meat 'look alike' dishes and Shanghainese classics like *xiao long bao*. The vegetable soup and fried noodles are especially delectable.

Red Pepper $$$ *7 Lan Fong Road, tel: 2577 3811, daily 11.30am–11.15pm.* This is the right place for those who like spicy food. Sichuan-style cuisine is served in a friendly, relaxed atmosphere. The staff will help you to order a meal that suits your taste; the eggplant (aubergine) with chilli and garlic and the sizzling chilli prawns are delicious.

ABERDEEN

Jumbo Floating Restaurant $$–$$$ *Aberdeen Harbour, tel: 2553 9111, www.jumbo.com.hk, Mon–Sat 11am–11.30pm, Sun 9am– 11.30pm.* This huge floating restaurant with fantastic decor has long been a tourist attraction. The fare includes seafood and other Cantonese dishes. It is certainly overrated, but it's a popular experience. There's a free shuttle boat from the Aberdeen promenade.

Top Deck At The Jumbo $$–$$$ *Jumbo Kingdom, Sham Wan Pier Drive, Aberdeen, tel: 2552 3331.* Disembark at the Jumbo when you see the golden dragons and head upstairs to the Top Deck. Decor is elegant oriental and the food is international – Asian and European dishes and buckets of fresh seafood. Perfect for a long lunch followed by drinks, lounging on sofas on the deck overlooking millionaires' yachts and humble *sampans*. Book ahead for weekend brunch buffet with free-flowing bubbly from 11.30am.

MACAU

Clube Militar de Macau $$$ *Av. da Praia Grande 795, tel: 853- 2871 4000, www.clubmilitardemacau.net, daily noon–3pm, 7– 11pm.* The atmospheric dining hall of the 1870 Clube Militar de Macau, with its high ceilings and arched windows, is a rare glimpse into the past. The extensive menu offers excellent Portuguese cuisine.

Nga Tim Café $$ *8 Rua Caetano, Coloane Village, Coloane, tel: 853-2888 2086, daily 11.30am–midnight.* Located on the central village square, in front of the Chapel of St Francis Xavier, this alfresco café is a place to kick back, take in old Macau and enjoy Chinese and Macanese classics.

O Porto Interior $$ *Rua do Almirante Sergio 259B, tel: 853-2896 7770, daily noon–11pm.* On the Inner Harbour, not far from the Maritime Museum, this restaurant is notable for its colonnaded facade and walls covered with azulejos and carved wooden grilles. The carefully prepared Macanese dishes are excellent value.

A–Z TRAVEL TIPS

A Summary of Practical Information

A

ACCOMMODATION (see also the list of Recommended Hotels, see page 132)

Hong Kong is home to some of the finest hotels in the world and most international chains have properties here. Service standards are generally high everywhere but rooms tend to be small except in the most expensive places. High- and mid-range hotels are all members of the Hong Kong Hotel Association (HKHA; www.hkha.org).

Advance reservations are essential for moderately priced hotels, and advisable for all others. For visitors arriving by air without reservations, there are two HKHA desks in arrivals that can arrange a room with any hotel associated with it. The service is provided free of charge and the desk is open from 6am–midnight.

Hong Kong's high seasons are October to early December, and March and April – trade fairs or local events such as Rugby 7s may fill hotels, so always check ahead. In quiet weeks in summer, prices may drop, and bonuses such as upgrades, free airport transport and discounts may be offered. For the best rates, check online and ask travel agents about packages that offer hotel and airfare.

Posted rates cover the room price only; a 10 percent service charge is added to the bill at check-out time.

AIRPORT

Arrival. International flights land at Hong Kong International Airport at Chek Lap Kok on Lantau Island, www.hkairport.com. Immigration and customs checks are efficient. Beyond the baggage inspection area you will find a bank, money changers, HKHA counters and two HKTB desks for tourist information. The Ground Transportation Centre is the place to go for information about transport into the city, or for taxis and limousine service.

Airport Express (AEL). (tel: 2881 8888; www.mtr.com.hk) This rail link is the best way to get into the city. Trains run every 12 minutes 5.54–12.48am daily to Kowloon (22 minutes) and Hong Kong station in Central (24 minutes). Tickets from automatic machines.

Airbuses. (tel: 2873 0818; https://nwstbus.com.hk) The buses serve all major hotels and most districts in Hong Kong. Take A21 to Kowloon, and A11 or A12 to Hong Kong Island. N21 and N11 operate the same routes after midnight. Travel time is about an hour. Buy tickets at the Commercial Service Counter or have exact fare ready.

Limousines and taxis. Major hotels operate their own limousine services; go to the HKHA desk, or look for hotel pick-up counters. If you take a taxi, you should be charged only what the meter reads, plus tolls and a charge for each piece of luggage placed in the boot.

Departure. All major airlines allow you to check in for your return flight at Hong Kong Central Station or Kowloon Station up to 24 hours before your departure. Boarding passes will be issued, and luggage transferred to the airport.

B

BUDGETING FOR YOUR TRIP

To give you an idea of what to expect, here are some average prices in Hong Kong dollars, but they should be regarded as approximate.

Airport transfer. Limousine from the airport to your hotel, about HK$500; taxis HK$250–400, plus tolls and luggage; Airport Express HK$90–100; Airbus HK$33–45.

Buses and trams. Buses HK$1.90–45, trams HK$2,3 for adults, HK$1,20 for children, minibuses and maxicabs HK$2–22.50, Peak Tram HK$28 (one way), HK$40 (return) for adults, HK$11 (one way), HK$18 (return) for children.

Car rental. A compact car costs around HK$750 a day. A car or limo with a driver costs around HK$160 an hour.

Ferries. Star Ferry HK$2.50; island ferries HK$10–31; Macau ferry HK$159–350.

Hotels. Luxury hotels range upwards from HK$2,500, top hotels from HK\$1,800; medium range hotels begin at around HK\$950, and inexpensive hotels less than HK\$950.

MTR. Mass Transit Railway fares range from HK\$3,5 to HK\$55.

Meals and drinks. In a moderately priced restaurant: set lunch HK\$80–150, dinner HK\$150–350; buffets are generally good value.

Taxis. HK\$17–22 for the first 2km (1.2 miles), HK\$1.40–1,60 for each succeeding 200m, HK\$20 for journeys via Cross Harbour Tunnel, HK\$30 via the Eastern Harbour Crossing, or HK\$40 via the Western Harbour Crossing (plus HK\$15 to cover driver's return toll), and HK\$5 for each piece of baggage.

Trains. From Kowloon to Lo Wu on the border with mainland China, first class HK\$77,5, standard class HK\$41,5.

C

CAR HIRE (See also Driving)

Driving in Hong Kong is not recommended. However, all international and many local hire firms operate in Hong Kong offering both self-drive and chauffeur-driven cars. Japanese, European and American models are available. Major credit cards are accepted. Drivers must be over 25 years old and have held a valid licence from their home country or an international licence for two years.

CLIMATE

The chart below gives an idea of average monthly temperatures in Hong Kong, and the number of rainy days per month. The best time to visit is October or November, when temperature and humidity drop and days are clear and sunny. From December until late February the air is moderately cool and humidity still low (around 73 percent). In spring humidity and temperature start rising. March and April can be very pleasant, but May to mid-September it's extremely hot and often wet, with most of the annual rainfall recorded during these months.

	J	F	M	A	M	J	J	A	S	O	N	D
°C	15	15	18	22	25	28	28	28	27	25	21	17
°F	59	59	64	72	77	82	82	82	81	77	70	63
Days of Rain												
	6	8	11	12	16	21	19	17	14	8	6	5

CLOTHING

From May to September you need lightweight summer clothing, and a raincoat and umbrella might come in handy. In restaurants and hotels air-conditioning can be fierce. From late September to early December shirt-sleeves and sweaters are appropriate, while from late December to February a warm jacket or light coat is advisable.

Informality is generally the rule. For sightseeing and shopping, shorts and T-shirts are acceptable in most places, but shorts, vests and flip-flops (thongs) are out of place in up-market restaurants and temples. Bring comfortable shoes for the steep slopes.

CONSULATES

Consulates are generally open Monday–Friday, 9am–noon and 2–4 or 5pm. Various sections may open at different hours, so call first.
Australia: 23rd floor, Harbour Centre, 25 Harbour Road, Wan Chai, tel: 2827 8881.
Canada: 9th floor, 25 Westlands Road, Quarry l, tel: 3719 4700.
New Zealand: 65th floor, Central Plaza, 18 Harbour Road, Wan Chai, tel: 2525 5044.
UK: 1 Supreme Court Road, Central, tel: 2901 3000.
US: 26 Garden Road, Central, tel: 2523 9011.

CRIME AND SAFETY (See also Emergencies)

Hong Kong is a safe city, night and day. The streets are usually full of people until late at night. Signs everywhere warn you to 'beware of pickpockets'. Be especially careful in busy markets, and on rush-hour buses and MTR trains. Leave your valuables in a hotel safe.

CUSTOMS AND ENTRY REQUIREMENTS

For most nationalities, only a passport is required for entry into Hong Kong. Subjects of the UK can stay up to six months without a visa; Canadians, Australians and New Zealanders and US citizens can stay for three months. To enter Macau, only a passport is needed, and most visitors can stay up to 20 days without a visa.

Visas are required for the People's Republic of China, so if you are taking any excursion over the border you will need a visa. Short-term tours to China may include visas; otherwise visas can be arranged at travel agents or China Travel Service (cts), 78–83 Connaught Road Central.

You can bring into Hong Kong duty-free: 19 cigarettes or 1 cigar or 25 grams of other tobacco, and 1 litre spirits (with above 30 percent vol). Firearms are strictly controlled, and can only be brought in by special permit. There are no currency restrictions.

D

DRIVING (See also Car hire)

Anyone over 18 with a valid licence and third-party insurance can drive in Hong Kong for 12 months without having to pay for a local licence (but you must be over 25 to hire a car). Drivers must carry a valid driver's licence and photo identification at all times.

Road conditions. Congestion is a serious problem in the city. Good highways connect to the New Territories and the airport.

Rules and regulations. Hong Kong traffic keeps to the left. All passengers are must wear seatbelts. Drivers may not use hand-held mobile phones. In China, cars keep to the right. The speed limit is 30mph (50kmh) in towns, elsewhere as marked.

Parking. This can be a headache, especially in the central areas, despite multistorey car parks. Most meters operate from 8am–midnight Monday–Saturday, and wardens are ever alert.

Breakdowns. Call the car hire firm. In an emergency, dial 999. Automobile Association: 391 Nathan Road, tel: 3583 3628.

Road signs. Most signs are standard international pictographs.

E

ELECTRICITY

Standard voltage is 220-volt, 50-cycle AC. Many hotels have razor fittings for all standard plugs and voltages. For other items, transformers and adapters are needed; you may need a plug for a laptop even if it is equipped to deal with both 220 and 110 volts. Most hotels supply hairdryers.

EMERGENCIES

Dial 999 for Police, Fire, or Ambulance departments. St John's Ambulance Brigade (www.stjohn.org.hk) is a free service, tel: 1878 000 on Hong Kong Island, in Kowloon, and in the New Territories. Hospitals with 24-hour emergency services are: Queen Mary Hospital, 102 Pokfulam Road, Hong Kong Island, tel: 2855 3838; Queen Elizabeth Hospital, 30 Gascoigne Road, Kowloon, tel: 2958 8888; and Hong Kong Adventist Hospital, 40 Stubbs Road, Hong Kong Island, tel: 3651 8888. Many hotels have doctors on call.

In Macau, dial 999 or 112 in an emergency.

G

GAY AND LESBIAN TRAVELLERS

Hong Kong is still fairly conservative, but there's a gay scene around Glenealy and Wyndham Street in Central Club 97 (www.epicurean. com.hk), Lan Kwai Fong on a Friday night is a good start. For more gay nightlife in Hong Kong www.travelgayasia.com

GETTING THERE

From the UK. CathayPacific (tel: 020-8834 8888; www.cathaypacific. com), British Airways (tel: 0844-4930 787; www.britishairways.com), and Virgin Atlantic Airways (tel: 0844-209 7777; www.virgin-atlantic. com) offer daily nonstop services from London to Hong Kong.

From Australia and New Zealand. Qantas (tel: 131 313; www. qantas.com.au) and Cathay Pacific (tel: 131 747) fly nonstop from Sydney and Melbourne. Air New Zealand (www.airnewzeland.co.nz) and Cathay Pacific (tel: 0800-800 454) non-stop from Auckland.

GUIDES AND TOURS

The Hong Kong Tourism Board (HKTB; www.discoverhongkong. com) organises a wide assortment of tours. Their 'Living Culture' and 'Nature' tours include a ride in Hong Kong's last genuine sailing junk, classes in tai chi, pearl and jade shopping, *feng shui*, as well as a guided hikes, birdwatching and visits to more remote corners. During the 'Wing Chu Experience' tour it is possible to learn some basic moves of this ancient Chinese martial art adopted and practiced by the kung fu legend and international movie star, Bruce Lee. Alternatively, you may want to take a bike tour to discover the untouched New Territories. Theme tours by HKTB include the outstanding 'Heritage Tour', to historic sites in the New Territories. 'Hong Kong Heritage Walk' lets you explore the colonial architectural heritage of Hong Kong on foot.

Tour operators include Gray Line Tours of Hong Kong Ltd., 5/F 72 Nathan Road, Tsim Sha Tsui, tel: 2368 7111, www.grayline.com. hk; Watertours, at 1023A, 10/F Star House, 3 Salisbury Road, Tsim Sha Tsui, tel: 2926 3868, www.watertours.com.hk, is the largest operator of boat and junk cruises; Splendid Tours and Travel Ltd, tel: 2316 2151, www.splendid.hk, has night cruises among its offerings; and China Travel Service of Hong Kong Ltd (CTS, www.ctshk.com) runs one- to three day tours of Guangzhou and other South China destinations.

Hong Kong Dolphinwatch Ltd., 1528 Star House, Tsim Sha Tsui, tel: 2984 1414; www.hkdolphinwatch.com, has a half-day eco-cruise to sight Hong Kong's threatened pink dolphins.

To hire a personal guide or a guide for a group, contact HKTB in Hong Kong, or CTS for guides in other South China destinations.

Rickshaws are no longer used for passengers, but HK$50 ($25 children buys a day pass for the double-decker open top Rickshaw Bus and hop-on-hop-off sightseeing tours around Central, Sheung Wan, Wan Chai and Causeway Bay (www.rickshawbus.com).

H

HEALTH AND MEDICAL CARE (See also Emergencies)

No vaccinations or special health precautions are needed. Food is safe, even in road side stalls, and you can safely drink the water, though most people prefer bottled water. Avoid eating locally caught shellfish and oysters; most restaurants use imported or farmed varieties. Wear a hat and use sunscreen, and always carry a bottle of water.

Travelling into China requires a few extra precautions. Drink only bottled water and use bottled or boiled water to brush your teeth. Don't eat raw food and choose fruit that can be peeled.

a bottle of drinking water **yat tchun soi**
I want to see a... **Ngor yiu tai...**
doctor **yee sang**
dentist **nga yee**

HOLIDAYS

Thanks to the convergence of British and Chinese traditions, Hong Kong celebrates 17 public holidays a year. Though banks and offices close, most shops and restaurants carry on as usual. At

Lunar New Year, many small family-run businesses close. Chinese holidays are fixed by the lunar calendar, so exact dates cannot be given.

January 1 New Year's Day

January or February Lunar New Year (3 days)

March or April Easter (Good Friday, Easter Monday)

April Ching Ming Festival

May 1 Labour Day

May Buddha's Birthday

May or June Tuen Ng (Dragon Boat) Festival

July 1 (or first weekday) Establishment Day of the Special Administrative Region

September Day following the mid-Autumn Festival

October 1 National Day

October Chung Yeung Festival

December 25 Christmas Day

December 26 Boxing Day

INTERNET

Free Wireless Broadband (WiFi) access is becoming more widespread in hotels, and the government's GovWiFi network provides free access via over 2000 hotspots at 400 locations, including public libraries, cultural and recreation centres, museums and parks.

LANGUAGE

The official languages of Hong Kong are English and Chinese. While Chinese can be called the world's most widely spoken language, it actually has innumerable dialects – people from Beijing can't understand a word that people from Hong Kong say; in fact they can't even understand what people from Shanghai say. What has bound the country together over thousands of years is the written language.

Each Chinese character represents an idea – a meaning, not a sound. There are about 50,000 characters, and some 5,000 of these are in common use. Chinese is traditionally written in columns, read from top to bottom and right to left, but today you often see printed Chinese characters presented much like a European language.

Putonghua, or Mandarin, is China's official language. Cantonese is spoken in Hong Kong and South China.

The following approximations of everyday Cantonese words and greetings may help:

Good morning **Jo sahn**
Good afternoon **Ng on**
Good evening **Mang on**
Good night **Jo tow**
Goodbye **Joy geen**
Please (for service) **M goi**
Please (invitation) **Ching**
Thank you (for service) **M goi**
Thank you (for a gift) **Daw jeh**
chop seal or stamp on a document
feng shui lucky siting of building or graves
gweilo Europeans, foreigners
hong big business firm
joss luck
yam seng 'cheers', 'bottoms up'

Getting around is difficult when place names are pronounced differently in English and Cantonese. Kowloon (Nine Dragons) sounds similar in both languages; here are some that differ:

Aberdeen **Heung Gong Jai**
Causeway Bay **Tung Lo Wan**
Central District **Jung Wan**
Cross Harbour Tunnel **Hoi Dai Sui Do**
Happy Valley **Pau Ma Dei**
Ocean Park **Hoi Yeung Gung Yuen**
The Peak **San Deng**
Peak Tram **Lam Che**
Repulse Bay **Chin Sui Wan**
Stanley **Chek Chue**
Star Ferry Pier **Tin Sing Ma Tau**

M

MEDIA

Newspapers and magazines. Local English-language dailies are the *South China Morning Post* and *The Standard*; the *China Daily* is a Hong Kong-published version of China's national English-language daily. The *International Herald Tribune*, edited in Paris, is printed simultaneously in Hong Kong six days a week.

Radio and television. Hong Kong has two free-to-air TV channels in English and, since 2014, four in Chinese. Six English-language radio channels provide a broad range, from easy listening to news. The BBC World Service broadcasts 24 hours a day at 675 kHz.

MONEY

Currency. Hong Kong's currency is freely convertible, and is pegged to the US dollar at a rate of around 7.8. The Hong Kong dollar is divided into 100 cents. Banknotes, in denominations of HK$10, HK$20, HK$50, HK$100, HK$500 and HK$1,000, are issued by three local banks, Hongkong and Shanghai Banking Corporation, the Bank of China and the Standard Chartered Bank. Coins, however, are minted by the Hong Kong government; they come in denominations of 10, 20 and 50 cents and HK$1, HK$2, HK$5 and HK$10. The image of the British queen has been replaced by the bauhinia tree flower, Hong Kong's regional emblem.

Currency in China and Macau. China's currency is *renminbi* (RMB) or *yuan*. In Shenzhen, Lo Wu stores will accept Hong Kong dollars and convert to RMB on the spot, but you may lose out. Taxis and other retailers want RMB so it may be worth changing money before crossing the border. In April 2014 HK$1 = RMB 0.79.

Macau's currency is the *pataca* and is completely interchangeable with Hong Kong dollars in Macau only.

Currency exchange. Foreign currencies can be exchanged at banks, hotels, money changers and major shopping outlets. Banks have better exchange rates, but charge a commission. Licensed money changers charge no commission, but the rates are about equivalent to a 5 percent commission. Money changers are found in all tourist areas and are open on holidays and late into the evening.

ATMs. ATMs are found all over Hong Kong and Macau. There are ATMs in Shenzhen, but these are harder to find.

Credit cards. Credit cards and charge cards are accepted everywhere you go in Hong Kong. Major hotels, restaurants and shops in China also accept the well-known credit cards.

Traveller's cheques. Can be exchanged at banks and most hotels. You must show your passport when you cash a cheque.

OPENING HOURS

Government offices open 9am–1pm and 2–5pm Monday–Friday.

Banking hours are usually 9am–4.30pm Monday–Friday. Some branches open 9am–12.30pm Saturday.

Business offices are normally open 9am–6pm Monday–Friday, lunch is 1–2pm. Most post offices open 9.30am–5.30pm Monday–

Friday. Central GPO and the post office at 10 Middle Road are open all day Saturday.

Most shops are open seven days a week. Shops on Hong Kong Island are open 10am–7pm in Central, 10am–9.30pm in Wan Chai, and 10am–10pm or later in Causeway Bay and Tsim Sha Tsui.

Museums open at 10 or 11am–6pm. Most close one day a week.

P

POST OFFICES

Post offices in Hong Kong deal with mailing letters, packages and provide a local and international courier service called Speedpost.

The main post office is on Hong Kong Island at 2 Connaught Place, near IFC, Monday–Saturday, 8am–6pm. In Kowloon, post offices are at 405 Nathan Road, between the Jordan and Yau Ma Tei underground stations, and at 10 Middle Road, one block north of Salisbury Road. For information, tel: 2921 2222, www.hongkongpost.com.

PUBLIC TRANSPORT

Hong Kong's public transport system is efficient and easy to use and remarkably inexpensive. Buses, ferries, and trams require the exact fare; the best option is an Octopus card (www.octopus.com.hk), purchased at MTR stations, 7–11 and Circle K stores and accepted on most buses and ferries, trams and the MTR system (including trains in the New Territories and the Airport Express Line). It costs HK$150 (including an HK$50 refundable deposit), and can be reloaded in units of HK$50 or HK$100 at MTR stations or convenience stores.

MTR. Hong Kong's Mass Transit Railway is one of the world's most modern, attractive, and easy-to-use undergrounds. It operates daily 6am–1am, and connects Kowloon, Hong Kong Island, the New Territories and Lantau. The lines (including the dedicated Disneyland Resort line) are colour-coded; signs and announcements are in English and Cantonese. Tickets for single fares, ranging from HK$4–26, can be purchased from vending machines. Take your ticket when it pops up on the turnstile, you will need it to exit at your destination.

Ferries. The Star Ferry (www.starferry.com.hk) is not just a means of transportation, but a not-to-be missed experience. It crosses Victoria Harbour, connecting Tsim Sha Tsui with Hong Kong Island at Central. It runs daily 6.30am–11.30pm every six to 12 minutes, and a token for the ferry costs HK$2 (HK$2,50 upper deck); passengers aged 65 or above (upon production of HKID or senior citizen card) go free.

Other ferries connecting sections of the city include: one from Central to Hung Hom; from Wan Chai to Tsim Sha Tsui and Sai Wan Ho to Kwun Tong.

Ferries to outlying islands are operated by New World First Ferry (for Lantau, Cheung Chau and Peng Chau, tel: 2131 8181) and Hong Kong and Kowloon Ferry (www.hkkf.com.hk; for Lamma, tel: 2815 6063). All depart from the Outlying Island Ferry Piers in front of the IFC buildings in Central. Fares vary, the highest being HK$31. Jetfoils and catamarans to Macau leave from the Macau Ferry Terminal in Sheung Wan every 15 minutes 7am–1am, every hour 1am–7am; one-way fares start at HK$138, and increase at night and at weekends.

Buses. The bus service in Hong Kong is good and relatively cheap. All bus stops have English route maps. Double-decker buses run 24 hours (night bus numbers are prefixed by an 'N') and cover even remote parts of Hong Kong. Fares range from HK$1.90–45, and the exact fare must be put in the box next to the driver (all buses accept Octopus cards). There are three companies: New World First Bus (tel: 2136 8888), Kowloon Motor Bus (KMB, tel: 2745 4466) and Citybus (tel: 2873 0818). Major terminals are on both sides of the Star Ferry, and on Hong Kong Island at Exchange Square.

'Public Light Buses' seat 16 passengers. You can hail them at designated stops but get off almost anywhere along their route. Tell the driver when you want to get off and pay as you leave. Minibuses are red and yellow, and you pay cash when you get off. Maxicabs are distinctive green-and-yellow vans that run set routes and you pay as you get on (they also take Octopus cards). The fares for both range from HK$2–22.50. Destinations are marked in English and Chinese on the front, but the English is often smaller and hard to read. Both ply routes around Hong Kong Island, and in Kowloon.

Trams. Hong Kong's picturesque double-decker trams are also a tourist attraction and provide a pleasant way to see the sights. They traverse the north coast of Hong Kong Island between Kennedy Town and Shau Kei Wan. Pick one up on Des Voeux, Queensway, or Hennessy roads. Enter at the rear and exit at the front, dropping HK$2.30 into the fare box as you leave. It's a flat rate regardless of the distance travelled. The service operates from 6am until midnight.

Trains. Hong Kong's rail link with China (formerly known as the Kowloon–Canton Railway, now part of the MTR system) runs 34km (21 miles) from Kowloon to the border. The local trains that serve commuters in the New Territories are an excellent way of visiting the area's towns and villages. Trains run daily every 3–10 minutes. Fares are very reasonable, costing HK$13 for standard class from Tsim Sha Tsui East to Sheung Shui and HK$26 for first class.

The MTR's Light Rail Transit system (LRT) operate in the western New Territories linking the towns of Tuen Mun and Yuen Long. Trains run Mon–Sat 5.30am–0.41am, 6am–midnight on Sunday.

Taxis. Hong Kong's metered taxis can be hailed on the street. Taxis on Hong Kong Island and Kowloon are red. Fares start at HK$17 for the first 2km (1.2 miles), and go up around HK$1.50 for every 200m; there are extra charges for luggage (HK$5 per piece) and trips through tunnels (see Budgeting for your Trip).

It's a good idea to have your destination and the name of your hotel written in Chinese. Many hotels print a list of well-known places in Chinese characters and English you can carry with you.

Funicular. The Peak Tram furnicular links Garden Road with Victoria Peak, daily 7am–midnight every 10 minutes. The climb to the Peak Tower takes eight minutes; from the top there's a panoramic view. The fare is HK$40 return for adults, HK$18 for children.

R

RELIGION

Confucianism, Buddhism and Taoism or a mixture thereof are the major religions in Hong Kong. There are also Christian churches of every denomination, Islamic mosques, Hindu temples and Jewish and Baha'i houses of worship. Anglican/Episcopal services are held at St John's Cathedral in Central, Hong Kong Island, and St Andrew's Church on Nathan Road, Kowloon. Catholic Mass is held at Rosary Chapel on South Chatham Road, Kowloon. For information, see the Saturday issue of the *South China Morning Post*.

Kowloon Mosque (Jamia Masjid), catering to Hong Kong's sizable Muslim population, is beside Kowloon Park, on Nathan Road.

T

TELEPHONE

Hong Kong's country code is 852; Macau's is 853. Both have 8-digit numbers. For overseas calls dial 001 (10011 for collect/reverse charge calls). For English-speaking information dial 1081; if you have difficulty in getting a number, dial 109. You can use a mobile if it is GSM900, PCS1800, CDMA or WCDMA; operators include Smartone-Vodaphone, 3, CSL and PCCW. All sell temporary SIM cards with reasonable rates for local calls and SMS. For IDD it's better to buy a calling card. International direct-dial calls can be made from any public phone, which require a HK$1, 2, 5 or 10 coins or a phone card. Hotels add a surcharge on both local and international calls.

TIME ZONES

The hours in the following chart refer to the months when many countries in the northern hemisphere move their clocks one hour ahead

(Daylight Savings). Hong Kong stays the same year-round, at GMT + 8.

New York	London	**Hong Kong**	Sydney	Auckland
7am	noon	**7pm**	9pm	11pm

TIPPING

Tipping in Hong Kong is confusing; who should be tipped and when is not always clear. Most hotels and restaurants add a 10 percent service charge, but whether it goes to staff is debatable, In inexpensive places, round up the bill or leave 5–10 percent.

Tourist guides do not indicate that they expect a tip, but they should receive about 10 percent of the cost of the tour. A hotel porter expects HK$5–10 per bag. Lavatory attendants deserve HK$2–5, depending on the establishment. For taxi drivers you can simply round up the fare to the nearest dollar or two.

The best rule is to tip according to how you feel; not everybody tips in Hong Kong and anything you give will be graciously received.

TOILETS

Public toilets are well dispersed and there are usually plenty of options. Shopping malls usually have good facilities and places frequented by tourists and up-market establishments will have Western toilets. You may encounter Chinese squat toilets in non-tourist areas or even in restaurants with a largely Chinese clientele; most of these in Hong Kong are clean and well-maintained.

Where are the toilets? **Chi saw haih been do a?**

TOURIST INFORMATION

The Hong Kong Tourism Board (HKTB) operates information and gift centres at key areas. There is one in the arrivals hall at Chek Lap

Kok, open daily 8am–9pm. The Hong Kong Island office is at The Peak Piazza (between The Peak Tower and The Peak Galleria), daily 11am–8pm. On the Kowloon side in Tsim Sha Tsui, there's an office on the Star Ferry Concourse, daily 8am–8pm. The HKTB Visitor Hotline, tel: 2508 1234, operates daily 9am–6pm, www.discoverhongkong.com.

The HKTB publishes free brochures and literature; the *Official Hong Kong Guide* is a monthly information booklet with an overview of attractions, shopping tips and current events and exhibitions. Free maps are available. There are several weekly and monthly publications, free at restaurants, bars and other outlets, including *Hong Kong Diary*, *BC* magazine (www.bcmagazine.net) and the *HK magazine* (http://hk-magazine.com) The *South China Morning Post* (www.scmp.com) has daily listings. A new arrival on the scene is the fortnightly *Time Out Hong Kong* (www.timeout.com.hk).

The Macau Government Tourist Office (MGTO; hotline tel: 2833 3000, www.macautourist.gov.mo) is at Chek Lap Kok, daily 9.30am–13pm, 14–17.45pm. MGTO offices are at both ends of the Macau ferry terminal: Room 336, 3/F, on the departure floor in Hong Kong, and in the arrivals hall at the Macau Ferry Terminal. Maps of Macau are available as well as *Macau Travel Talk* and the pamphlet *Macau Walking Tours*. Some brochures are available online.

Overseas HKTB branch offices: Australia: Hong Kong House, Level 4, 80 Druitt Street, Sydney, NSW 2000, tel: 02-9283 3083. UK: 6 Grafton Street. London WIX 3LB, tel: 020-7533 7100.

TRAVELLERS WITH DISABILITIES

Hong Kong is not an easy place for travellers with disabilities. Hong Kong's frequent steps and many steep streets, narrow crowded footpaths and the pedestrian overpasses are not easily negotiated. Some hotels have special facilities for the disabled, most buildings have lifts, escalators are common, and taxis are inexpensive and easy to find. Contact HKTB (www.wheelawaydisabledtravel.com) for more information and advice.

WEBSITES

www.discoverhongkong.com – HKTB's website.
www.lcsd.gov.hk – Leisure and Cultural Services Department of the
Hong Kong Government
www.macautourism.gov.mo – Macau's tourist information.
www.travelocity.com – air fares and bookings and accommodation.
www.bestfares.com – for airfares

WEIGHTS AND MEASURES

The international metric system is in official use. However, Imperial
and Chinese measurements are still commonly used. Food products
are generally sold by the kg, lb or *catty* (1.3lbs/600g). Market stalls
and stores will give you a tape measure if needed. Clothes and shoes
are in a mix of Asian, European, American and British sizes.

YOUTH HOSTELS

Youth hostels are located in remote scenic areas, but easily acces-
sible by public transport. Main hostels are Jockey Club Mount Davis
Youth Hostel, Mt Davis Path, Mt Davis, Western District, tel: 2817
5715; and Bradbury Jockey Club, 66 Ting Kok Road, Tai Mei Tuk,
Tai Po, New Territories, tel: 2662 5123. For information, contact the
Youth Hostels Association, tel: 2788 1638, www.yha.org.hk.

Centrally located budget establishments with simple or bunk-
bed rooms include HK Star World Guest House, Unit J, 9/F, Wing
Lee Building, 27-33 Kimberley Road, Tsim Sha Tsui, tel: 2368 5509;
www.hkstarworldguestehouse.com; and the YWCA's Garden View
International House, overlooking the botanical gardens at 1 Mac-
Donnell Road, Central, tel: 2877 3737; http://hotel.ywca.org.hk, de-
scribes itself as a 4-star hotel and the prices are similar.

Recommended Hotels

Hong Kong has some of the most luxurious hotels in the world, with properties belonging to nearly all the major international chains. The city welcomes almost 30 million visitors a year, half of whom are from mainland China. Hotels listed below have full air-conditioning, offer 24-hour or more limited room service, and a wide range of facilities. Hong Kong hotels have excellent business services and conference facilities, and many have acclaimed restaurants.

Reservations are strongly recommended, particularly at Christmas, Chinese New Year, during major trade fairs and China's golden week following 1 May and 1 October. If you do arrive without a reservation, the Hong Kong Hotel Association (www.hkha.org) at the airport can arrange accommodation with its members.

As a basic guide, the symbols below have been used to indicate high-season rates in Hong Kong dollars, based on double occupancy. A 10 percent service charge will be added to the bill. In Macau, there's a 10 percent service charge and a 5 percent government tax. All Macau hotels charge high rates for Friday and Saturday night stays.

$$$$	above HK$2,500
$$$	HK$1,600–HK$2,500
$$	HK$950–HK$1,600
$	below HK$950

CENTRAL

Bishop Lei International House $$ *4 Robinson Road, Mid-Levels, tel: 2868 0828, www.bishopleihtl.com.hk.* An excellent-value option, owned by the Catholic Diocese of Hong Kong and located 15 minutes' walk from the nightlife hub of Lan Kwai Fong. SoHo is on its doorstep via the Mid-Levels Escalator. There's nothing remarkable about the decor, but it offers many of the facilities of an upper-range hotel – including a gym, pool, free in-room broadband, 24-hour room service and babysitter and concierge services – at exceptionally reasonable prices. Some suites even have impressive harbour views.

Four Seasons $$$$ *8 Finance Road, Central, tel: 3196 8888,* www.fourseasons.com/hongkong. This five-star hotel has rooms with wall-to-wall windows giving spectacular harbour views, and decorated in contemporary style with wood and silk wall panelling. The hotel has an indoor link to the Airport Express station building and the IFC Mall, stocked with upmarket shopping, a great cinema and restaurants. 399 rooms and suites.

Hotel LKF $$$$ *33 Wyndham Street, Lan Kwai Fong, tel: 3518 9333;* www.hotel-lkf.com.hk. One of the city's hippest addresses, on Wyndham Street, right in the middle of Lan Kwai Fong. The sleek, minimalist rooms have espresso machines and DVD players, and guests can avail themselves of a whole range of services. Dining facilities include a very sexy 29th-floor cocktail bar and supper lounge, AZURE, which is where breakfast is served. Great hotel, although note that the streets outside can be noisy into the small hours.

Island Shangri-La, Hong Kong $$$$ *Pacific Place, Supreme Court Road, tel: 2877 3838,* www.shangri-la.com. On arrival, the outstanding feature here is a 17-storey atrium with abundant greenery. Large rooms with oversize bathrooms have views of the harbour or hillside. Outstanding Cantonese, French and Japanese restaurants and fine seafood at The Lobster Bar. Outdoor swimming pool and a 24-hour gym. 565 rooms.

Traders Hotel $$ *508 Queen's Road West, Sheung Wan, Western District, tel: 2974 1234,* www.shangri-la.com. A comfortable, excellent-value mid-range hotel in the oldest district on Hong Kong Island. A rooftop pool and swish Sky Lounge on the 28th floor both enjoy superior views. Ten minutes' drive from Central but a courtesy shuttle bus is provided to the MTR and Airport Express stations. 280 rooms, three of them with facilities for guests with disabilities.

CAUSEWAY BAY/WAN CHAI

Empire Hotel $$ *8 Wing Hing Street, Causeway Bay, tel: 3692 2333*, www.empirehotel.com.hk. A good-value hotel located close to Victoria Park, near Tin Hau MTR and Kings Road trams so it is easy to reach Causeway Bay and Wan Chai shopping and night-life district. As the newest of three Empires in Hong Kong, this property has a business lounge and spa. Rooms are on the small side, but there is a 42-inch flat screen TV and for added entertainment, the glass walls in the bathroom turn opaque at the flick of a switch. 280 rooms.

The Excelsior $$$ *281 Gloucester Road, Causeway Bay, tel: 2894 8888*, www.mandarinoriental.com. Busy hotel in excellent location near Victoria Park and bustling Causeway Bay. Guest rooms are plush and comfortable with views over the harbour or park. Italian and Cantonese restaurants and a sociable English-style pub in the basement. 884 rooms and suites.

The Fleming $$–$$$ *41 Fleming Road, Wan Chai, tel: 3607 2288*, www.thefleming.com.hk. When location is everything, this 66-room boutique hotel in the middle of the Wan Chai commercial and nightlife district does the trick. Compact but cosy stylish rooms packed with gadgets and thoughtful touches, such as a female-only floor and free access to California Fitness next door. Some rooms have kitchenettes.

Grand Hyatt Hong Kong $$$$ *1 Harbour Road, Wan Chai, tel: 2588 1234*, www.hongkong.grand.hyatt.com. A futuristic design of marble and glass, magnificent views over the harbour, and an Art-Deco style interior characterise this fine hotel. The rooms are smart and contemporary with luxurious amenities. The Hyatt's award-winning Plateau Spa has dedicated spa suites where you can stay for maximum relaxation and pampering. 539 rooms.

Novotel Century Hong Kong $$ *238 Jaffe Road, tel: 2598 8888,* www.accorhotels.com. A solid four-star establishment. This 23-storey hotel is a short walk via covered walkway to the Convention and Exhibition Centre and is convenient for Wan Chai and MTR. 512 rooms.

Park Lane $$$ *310 Gloucester Road, Causeway Bay, tel: 2293 8888,* www.parklane.com.hk. Across from Victoria Park, this attractive hotel with modern marble decor is close to restaurants, shops, department stores and nightlife. 803 rooms.

Renaissance Harbour View $$$ *1 Harbour Road, Wan Chai, tel: 2802 8888,* www.renaissancehotels.com. This spectacular hotel adjoins the Convention and Exhibition Centre on the Wan Chai waterfront. About half of the rooms have harbour views. There are Cantonese, Continental and international restaurants. 862 rooms and suites.

KOWLOON

Eaton Hotel Hong Kong $$ *380 Nathan Road, Yau Ma Tei, tel: 2782 1818,* www.eaton-hotel.com. Extremely pleasant hotel with facilities including an attractive outdoor pool and service that rates well above its category. The emphasis is on contemporary styling and good value, and prices are very competitive. Well positioned for trawling markets, shops and cinemas, and halfway between Yau Ma Tei and Jordan MTR station. 465 rooms.

Holiday Inn Golden Mile $$$ *50 Nathan Road, Tsim Sha Tsui, tel: 2369 3111,* www.ichotelsgroup.com. This hotel is conveniently located in the midst of Nathan Road's 'Golden Mile' shopping. The rooms are a good size and modern, with floor-to-ceiling windows that give views of Kowloon's packed streets and tenement buildings. 585 rooms.

InterContinental Grand Stanford Hotel $$$ *70 Mody Road, Tsim Sha Tsui East, tel: 2721 5161,* www.hongkong.intercontinental. com. On the waterfront, with views over the harbour, this hotel is less glamourous than its sister hotel on the TST waterfront but it provides top service and accommodation at a more reasonable price. About half the rooms have harbour views. There are Italian and Cantonese restaurants. Attractive outdoor pool area. 570 rooms.

InterContinental Hong Kong $$$$ *18 Salisbury Road, Kowloon, tel: 2721 1211*, www.hongkong-ic.intercontinental.com. One of Hong Kong's top hotels, set on the waterfront, with luxurious granite and marble decor and harbour views. Guest rooms have spacious Italian marble bathrooms. Service throughout is excellent and the hotel is home to Hong Kong's first celebrity chef restaurants – Nobu and Spoon. 590 rooms.

Kowloon Hotel $$$ *19–21 Nathan Road, Tsim Sha Tsui, tel: 2929 2888*, www.thekowloonhotel.com. Tucked just behind the Peninsula, the Kowloon's rooms are small and the absence of a pool keeps prices low and good value. Guests take a shuttle to swim at the sister property, Harbour Plaza Metropolis, or more conveniently, pay HK$150 to use the up-market YMCA in the next block. 736 rooms.

Kowloon Shangri-La $$$ *64 Mody Road, Tsim Sha Tsui East, tel: 2721 2111*, www.shangri-la.com. Relaxed atmosphere and good service in this hotel. Rooms are large and luxurious; some have harbour views. Nadaman restaurant offers award-winning Japanese cuisine and Michelin two-star Shang Palace Cantonese specialities. Superb Italian food at Angelini. 688 rooms and suites.

Langham Place $$$$ *555 Shanghai Street, Mong Kok, tel: 3552 3388*, http://hongkong.langhamplacehotels.com. A modern five-star hotel in the heart of crowded Mong Kok, Langham Place prides itself on its use of technology, and shows a softer side with great artwork throughout the building. Rooms have floor-to-ceiling windows and contemporary furnishings. Stylish touches include a heated roof-top pool, Chinese-themed Chuan spa and free Wi-Fi in a laid back business centre that merges into its lounge bar. 666 rooms.

Marco Polo Gateway $$$ *Harbour City, 3 Canton Road, Tsim Sha Tsui, tel: 2113 0888*, www.marcopolohotels.com. One of a trio of Marco Polo hotels, this one is located in the Harbour City shopping complex, a step from the Star Ferry terminal; others are the higher-priced Hong Kong Hotel and the Prince. Good-sized rooms. 400 rooms.

The Mira $$ *118 Nathan Road, Tsim Sha Tsui, tel: 2368 1111*, www.themirahotel.com. After a US$65-million makeover in 2009, The Mira is a design-conscious hotel with a fresh attitude and bold designs. Enjoys a great location in the heart of Tsim Sha Tsui, with some rooms looking towards Kowloon Park. Close to Knutsford Terrace dining area.

Nathan Hotel $ *378 Nathan Road, Yau Ma Tei, tel: 2388 5141*, www.nathanhotel.com. This quiet and pleasant hotel near the Temple Street Night Market has spacious, nicely decorated no-frills rooms. The Penthouse restaurant serves Cantonese and Western food. Business centre. 189 rooms.

Novotel Hong Kong $$–$$$ *Nathan Road Kowloon, 348 Nathan Road, Yau Ma Tei, tel: 3965 8888*, www.novotel.com. Smart contemporary hotel that offers extremely comfortable accommodation with some neat touches. Strong images of Hong Kong Skyline decorate guest rooms and there are iMacs for guests' use in the lobby area. It's close to MTR stations and well-located for exploring the city. 389 rooms.

Peninsula $$$$ *Salisbury Road, Tsim Sha Tsui, tel: 2920 2888*, http://hongkong.peninsula.com. Hong Kong's most historic hotel, first opened in 1928, is a study in colonial elegance. The famous English-style afternoon tea in the lobby is a must for visitors. Guest rooms in the newer 32-storey tower offer spectacular views; furnishings and amenities are sumptuous, and service is of the highest standard. Gaddi's is Hong Kong's premier French restaurant, while other fine choices offer Pacific Rim, continental, Swiss, Japanese and Cantonese cuisine. There are top business and fitness facilities, too. 300 rooms.

Royal Garden $$$–$$$$ *69 Mody Road, Tsim Sha Tsui East, tel: 2721 5215*, www.rghk.com.hk. An attractive hotel with pool, tennis court, gym, garden and a putting green on its rooftop Sky Clubs. The 25m pool is open-air but heated when the weather is cool. Guest rooms open onto terraces overlooking a plant-filled 15-storey atrium with pools and waterfalls. The rooms are cosy, elegant and inviting, and the most expensive ones have harbour views. There are 37-inch or 46-inch plasma TV screens in each guest room. There are Italian, Cantonese and Japanese restaurants, as well as a restaurant in the atrium. 420 rooms, including 48 suites.

Royal Pacific Hotel and Towers $$–$$$ *33 Canton Road, Tsim Sha Tsui, tel: 2736 1188*, www.royalpacific.com.hk. Located in China Hong Kong City, which also houses the Hong Kong China Ferry terminal, this no-frills hotel is extremely convenient for trips to Macau or Southern China and is just over the road from Kowloon Park. Rooms in the Hotel Wing overlook the park, while those in the Towers Wing have views of Victoria Harbour. 673 rooms and suites.

Salisbury YMCA $ *41 Salisbury Road, Tsim Sha Tsui, tel: 2268 7000*, www.ymcahk.org.hk. You should reserve well in advance for this hotel, which is located next door to the Peninsula. It's one of the best bargains in Hong Kong, offering the facilities and service of far more expensive hotels at a fraction of the cost. The rooms are simple in decor, but are comfortable and well-equipped. There are restaurant and food outlets, plus two swimming pools, a fitness gym and sports centre with squash courts and a climbing wall. 363 rooms and suites, 7 dorms.

Sheraton Hong Kong Hotel and Towers $$$$ *20 Nathan Road, Tsim Sha Tsui, tel: 2369 1111*, www.sheraton.com/hongkong. Located near the harbour front and the Space Museum and Art Museum. The decor is contemporary with Asian motifs. The guest rooms facing the harbour have great views. Restaurants include a Japanese one, an oyster bar and Celestial Court Chinese restaurant. 782 rooms.

NEW TERRITORIES

Royal Park $$ *8 Pak Hok Ting Street, Sha Tin, tel: 2601 2111,* www.royalpark.com.hk. This hotel near Sha Tin's New Town Plaza shopping complex is easily accessed from the city by MRT or the hotel's own shuttle bus to Tsim Sha Tsui. The Royal Park served as an Olympic village when Hong Kong hosted the 2008 Olympic equestrian events. The rooms have marble-tiled bathrooms and views over Shatin Central Park and the Shing Mun River. There are indoor and outdoor pools, plus special facilities for guests with disabilities. 443 rooms.

Silvermine Beach Resort $–$$ *D.D. 2 Lot ilvermine Bay, Mui Wo, Lantau, tel: 6810 0111,www.silvermineresort.com.* A pleasant if basic hotel overlooking Silvermine Bay on Lantau Island, a half-hour ferry ride from Central, and convenient for buses to fine beaches, country walks and the Big Buddha. Some of the rooms overlook the beach, others the mountains or the garden. There is also a coffee shop and Chinese restaurant. The hotel has an outdoor swimming pool, gym and sauna. 128 rooms.

MACAU

Altira $$$ *Avenida de Kwong Tung, Taipa, tel: 853-2886 8888,* www.altiramacau.com. One of the new breed of integrated casino resorts in the MSAR, Crown Macau opened in May 2007, raising the bar by promising 6-star service. There are Japanese, Chinese and Italian restaurants, two cafés, the great Altira spa and extremely spacious rooms. 216 rooms.

Pousada de Coloane $$ *Praia de Cheoc Van, Coloane, tel: 853-2888 2143,* www.hotelpcoloane.com.mo. Quiet, family-run hotel in a nice spot by the beach. Decor is rustic Portuguese, with blue-and-white wall tiles *(azulejos)* and terracotta tiles on the floor. It's nothing fancy, but there is a small swimming pool with a slide for children. The Pousada's beautiful terrace is a lovely place to slow down, relax, eat home-style Portuguese food, and enjoy the views of Cheoc Van beach. 28 rooms.

INDEX

Berlitz pocket guide

Hong Kong

Thirteenth edition 2014

Written by Alice Fellows
Updated by Maciej Zglinicki
Edited by Sarah Clark
Picture Editor: Tom Smyth
Art Editor: Shahid Mahmood
Series Editor: Tom Stainer
Production: Rebeka Davies

Photography credits: 123RF 52; Alex Havret/
Apa Publications 3T, 3BR, 5M, 5T, 5CT, 19, 38,
54, 56, 87, 90, 92; Glyn Genin/Apa Publications
72, 73; HKTB 40, 64; Hong Kong Dance
Company 88; Langham Hotels 4/5M; Ming
Tang-Evans/Apa Publications 1, 2TC, 2MC,
2ML, 2TL, 3M, 3TC, 3M, 3BL, 4ML, 4TL, 4ML,
4TL, 6ML, 6TL, 6ML, 7MC, 7MC, 7TC, 8, 11, 12,
21, 22, 24, 26, 28, 29, 31, 32, 33, 34, 37, 43, 44,
46, 48, 49, 50, 57, 58, 60, 61, 62, 63, 66, 68, 71,
74, 75, 76, 77, 78, 80, 83, 85, 93, 94, 97, 98, 99,
100, 102; Public domain 15, 17; Yadid Levy/Apa
Publications 5MC
Cover picture: Fotolia

Every effort has been made to provide
accurate information in this publication,
but changes are inevitable. The publisher
cannot be responsible for any resulting
loss, inconvenience or injury.

Contact us

At Berlitz we strive to keep our guides as
accurate and up to date as possible, but if you
find anything that has changed, or if you have
any suggestions on ways to improve this guide,
then we would be delighted to hear from you.

Berlitz Publishing, PO Box 7910,
London SE1 1WE, England.
email: berlitz@apaguide.co.uk
www.insightguides.com/berlitz

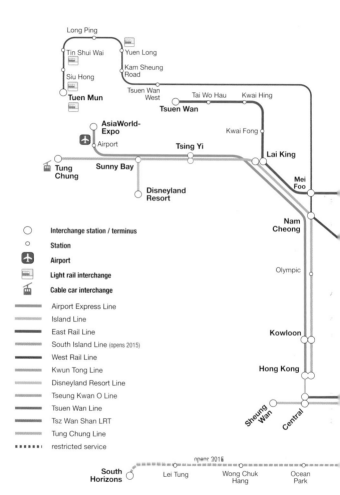

Long Ping

Tin Shui Wai

Yuen Long

Kam Sheung
Road

Siu Hong

Tsuen Wan
West

Tuen Mun

Tai Wo Hau

Kwai Hing

Tsuen Wan

**AsiaWorld-
Expo**

Airport

Kwai Fong

Tsing Yi

Lai King

**Tung
Chung**

Sunny Bay

Mei
Foo

Disneyland
Resort

**Nam
Cheong**

Olympic

○	Interchange station / terminus
o	Station
✈	Airport
🚃	Light rail interchange
🚡	Cable car interchange
	Airport Express Line
	Island Line
	East Rail Line
	South Island Line (opens 2015)
	West Rail Line
	Kwun Tong Line
	Disneyland Resort Line
	Tseung Kwan O Line
	Tsuen Wan Line
	Tsz Wan Shan LRT
	Tung Chung Line
▪▪▪▪▪▪▪	restricted service

Kowloon

Hong Kong

**Sheung
Wan**

Central

opens 2016

**South
Horizons**

Lei Tung

Wong Chuk
Hang

Ocean
Park

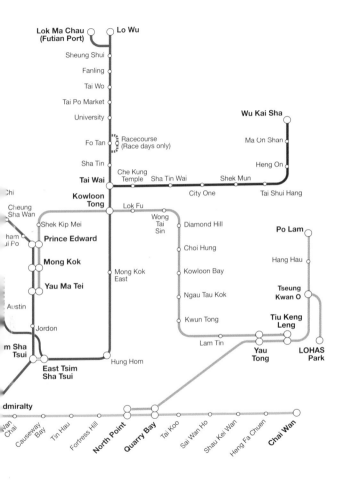

Berlitz®

speaking your language

phrase book & dictionary
phrase book & CD

Available in: Arabic, Brazilian Portuguese*, Burmese*, Cantonese
Chinese, Croatian, Czech*, Danish*, Dutch, English, Filipino, Finnish*, French,
German, Greek, Hebrew*, Hindi*, Hungarian*, Indonesian, Italian, Japanese,
Korean, Latin American Spanish, Malay, Mandarin Chinese, Mexican Spanish,
Norwegian, Polish, Portuguese, Romanian*, Russian, Spanish, Swedish, Thai,
Turkish, Vietnamese
*Book only